WATERSHED MANAGEMENT

WATERSHED MANAGEMENT

MR. PAWAR RAJENDRA ANNA MR. SONAWANE AKASH SANKAR MS. TRIBHUVAN LEENA KERU

WATERSHED MANAGEMENT

MR. PAWAR RAJENDRA ANNA MR. SONAWANE AKASH SANKAR MS.
TRIBHUVAN LEENA KERU

Contents

Foreword

A Foreword is a short introduction to the book, usually by a person other than the author. The purpose of the Foreword is to introduce the author or his work.

A Foreword could talk about why the book's content is relevant in its current scenario or how it created a historical impact when it was first released or the importance of the author's work.

As you can see here, the first paragraph is usually given a Watershed is a topographically delineated area drained by a stream system i.e. the total land area above some point on a stream or river that drains down slope to the lowest point The first paragraph of a new section after a subheading should also be given a Watershed Management. This rule applies to all chapters in the book.

Headers in the front matter of the book contain the name of the chapter alone. Pages in which the chapter starts would not have headers or footers.

The Foreword is usually signed by its writer with his credentials and the date. You can delete this page if you do not wish to include a Foreword in the book.

We've added additional text in this section to show you how the headers and footers appear in the subsequent pages. Please delete the instructions and the additional text when you add the actual content of the book.

When written by the author, the foreword may cover the story of how the book came into being or how the idea for the book was developed, and may include thanks and acknowledgments to people who were helpful to the author during the time of writing. Unlike a preface, a foreword is always signed.

Name of the author of the Foreword

Credentials

Date

Preface

Preface

The Preface is an introductory passage to the book, which is written by the author. It could talk about how the story came into being, the purpose of the book, its main characters, the author's journey of writing the book, etc.

As you can see here, the first paragraph is usually given a flush left alignment (Normal_without indent) and all subsequent paragraphs are given a slight indent (Normal_indent). The first paragraph of a new section after a subheading should also be given a flush left alignment. This rule applies to all chapters in the book.

Headers in the front matter of the book contain the name of the chapter alone. Pages in which the chapter starts would not have headers or footers.

The Preface is usually signed by the author with the date. You can delete this page if you wish to not include a Preface in the book.

We've added additional text in this section to show you how the headers and footers appear in the subsequent pages. Please delete the instructions and the additional text when you add the actual content of the book.

Lorem ipsum dolor sit amet, consectetur adipiscing elit. Sed ornare tristique mauris at varius. Phasellus arcu leo, tristique quis nulla id, ultrices varius diam. Morbi vulputate lacinia odio, sed tristique est sollicitudin a. Nullam fringilla dui sit amet pretium facilisis. Ut in neque dui. Aliquam vehicula sem id gravida finibus. Pellentesque sodales efficitur arcu, at dapibus enim porta vitae. Duis porttitor euismod eros elementum auctor. Praesent libero tortor, gravida ac fringilla sed, lobortis a dui. Nullam bibendum condimentum urna. Duis tincidunt imperdiet ipsum, vitae feugiat urna. Nulla facilisi. Curabitur ut ultricies justo, ac pretium sem. Aliquam aliquet ipsum quis tortor ultrices, vitae posuere orci porta.

Curabitur dignissim risus vitae felis lobortis vehicula. In tempus tincidunt diam, vel malesuada leo fringilla nec.

Fusce laoreet ipsum sem, a vestibulum turpis vestibulum et. Donec venenatis finibus tincidunt. Quisque placerat tellus lectus, eu consequat tellus suscipit vitae. Curabitur pharetra libero diam, at imperdiet dolor malesuada congue. Sed ac consectetur elit. Suspendisse eu faucibus quam. Mauris volutpat molestie urna. Duis vestibulum ante vel odio efficitur, vehicula euismod ex malesuada.

Author name

Date

Acknowledgements

Acknowledgments

The Acknowledgments page is usually written by the author to publically thank people who have contributed to the book.

Acknowledgments in some books run on for pages, but it is generally considered good practice to limit this section to a page, so that readers are not tempted to overlook it entirely.

As you can see here, the first paragraph is usually given a flush left alignment (Normal_without indent) and all subsequent paragraphs are given a slight indent (Normal_indent). The first paragraph of a new section after a subheading should also be given a flush left alignment. This rule applies to all chapters in the book.

Headers in the front matter of the book contain the name of the chapter alone. Pages in which the chapter starts would not have headers or footers.

You can delete this page if you do not wish to include an Acknowledgments page in the book.

We've added additional text in this section to show you how the headers and footers appear in the subsequent pages. Please delete the instructions and the additional text when you add the actual content of the book.

Lorem ipsum dolor sit amet, consectetur adipiscing elit. Sed ornare tristique mauris at varius. Phasellus arcu leo, tristique quis nulla id, ultrices varius diam. Morbi vulputate lacinia odio, sed tristique est sollicitudin a. Nullam fringilla dui sit amet pretium facilisis. Ut in neque dui. Aliquam vehicula sem id gravida finibus. Pellentesque sodales efficitur arcu, at dapibus enim porta vitae. Duis porttitor euismod eros elementum auctor. Praesent libero tortor, gravida ac fringilla sed, lobortis a dui. Nullam bibendum condimentum urna. Duis tincidunt imperdiet ipsum, vitae feugiat urna. Nulla facilisi. Curabitur ut ultricies justo, ac pretium sem.

Aliquam aliquet ipsum quis tortor ultrices, vitae posuere orci porta. Curabitur dignissim risus vitae felis lobortis vehicula. In tempus tincidunt diam, vel malesuada leo fringilla nec.

Fusce laoreet ipsum sem, a vestibulum turpis vestibulum et. Donec venenatis finibus tincidunt. Quisque placerat tellus lectus, eu consequat tellus suscipit vitae. Curabitur pharetra libero diam, at imperdiet dolor malesuada congue. Sed ac consectetur elit. Suspendisse eu faucibus quam. Mauris volutpat molestie urna. Duis vestibulum ante vel odio efficitur, vehicula euismod ex malesuada.

Prologue

Introduction

A Prologue, in case of fiction books, can be an excerpt from the book or a section of the story that happens before the true beginning of the story. It could provide readers an introduction to the nature of the characters in the story, a view of events that happened earlier and also set the tone of the book.

An Introduction, in case of non-fiction books, defines what the book is about, what a reader can expect from the book, the motivation for the book and, sometimes, guidance on how to use the book.

As you can see here, the first paragraph is usually given a flush left alignment (Normal_without indent) and all subsequent paragraphs are given a slight indent (Normal_indent). The first paragraph of a new section after a subheading should also be given a flush left alignment. This rule applies to all chapters in the book.

Headers in the front matter of the book contain the name of the chapter alone. Pages in which the chapter starts would not have headers or footers.

You can delete this page if you do not wish to have a Prologue or Introduction in the book.

We've added additional text in this section to show you how the headers and footers appear in the subsequent pages. Please delete the instructions and the additional text when you add the actual content of the book.

Lorem ipsum dolor sit amet, consectetur adipiscing elit. Sed ornare tristique mauris at varius. Phasellus arcu leo, tristique quis nulla id, ultrices varius diam. Morbi vulputate lacinia odio, sed tristique est sollicitudin a. Nullam fringilla dui sit amet pretium facilisis. Ut in neque dui. Aliquam vehicula sem id gravida finibus. Pellentesque sodales efficitur arcu, at dapibus enim porta vitae.

Duis porttitor euismod eros elementum auctor. Praesent libero tortor, gravida ac fringilla sed, lobortis a dui. Nullam bibendum condimentum urna. Duis tincidunt imperdiet ipsum, vitae feugiat urna. Nulla facilisi. Curabitur ut ultricies justo, ac pretium sem. Aliquam aliquet ipsum quis tortor ultrices, vitae posuere orci porta. Curabitur dignissim risus vitae felis lobortis vehicula. In tempus tincidunt diam, vel malesuada leo fringilla nec.

Fusce laoreet ipsum sem, a vestibulum turpis vestibulum et. Donec venenatis finibus tincidunt. Quisque placerat tellus lectus, eu consequat tellus suscipit vitae. Curabitur pharetra libero diam, at imperdiet dolor malesuada congue. Sed ac consectetur elit. Suspendisse eu faucibus quam. Mauris volutpat molestie urna. Duis vestibulum ante vel odio efficitur, vehicula euismod ex malesuada.

Content

CHAPTER ONE

Concept of watershed management

- Definition, concepts of watershed; watershed management, Principle of watershed management
- Necessity of watershed management
- Problems in watershed management

INTRODUCTION

In order to understand the concept of watershed, you may go out when it is raining. You would observe that during rains, water flows here and there and eventually follows a particular path. Finally, it gets collected at a particular point (particularly lowest point in your area) depending on the slope. The area which contributes water and flows to the lowest point resembles the watershed. The rainwater falling on a roof always flows through a particular outlet (spout). Taking spout as a point/outlet, the area of the roof may be termed as a watershed. If you have separate spouts for different roofs in your house, you may have many small watersheds within your house. The term watershed consists of two words: water and shed. Water occurs in nature mostly in solid, liquid and vapour forms. In watershed, water is considered mainly in liquid form. The word "shed" refers to the roof of a shed which collects rainwater and drains out. Shed thus can be defined as an area well marked by a boundary which receives rainwater and drains out towards a common drainage point or outlet. In the next unit, role of watershed management, its components, major characteristics and criteria for selection of watershed will be dealt with. Integrated watershed management and the importance of institutional arrangement were also highlighted.

DEFINITION OF WATERSHED

Watershed is a topographically delineated area drained by a stream system i.e. the total land area above some point on a stream or river that drains down slope to the lowest point. The watershed is a hydrologic unit often used as physical unit, biological unit and a socio-economic political unit for planning and management of natural resources. Watershed may also be defined as a natural unit of land which collects water and drains through a common point called an outlet by a system of drains. Therefore, watershed is the area encompassing the catchments, command and delta area of a stream. The top most portion of the watershed is known as "ridge" and a line joining the ridge portion along the boundary of the watershed is called as "ridgeline". A watershed is thus a logical unit for planning optimal development of its soil, water and biomass resources.

Scope of Watershed Management

As we have already seen in the previous section, watersheds represent small basins. By delineating the ridgelines in a medium or a large river basin, the entire basin can be subdivided into a number of watersheds, each with an area within 2,000 km2. Because of their compact size, it is always easier to manage watersheds rather than a river basin. In a well-managed watershed, all the natural resources such as soil, water, vegetation, etc. are conserved. Vegetation or plants play a vital role in conserving the natural resources of a watershed such as soil and water. The underground components of the plants such as roots spread within the soil and thereby stabilize and reinforce the soil. This generally leads to soil conservation. The water infiltrates below the ground through the voids in the soil as well as through the interface between the root surface and the soil. The terrestrial components of plants such as stems, branches and leaves prevent the soil below it from getting directly exposed to sunlight as well as to the impact of raindrops. Thus, a significant part of the momentum and energy in rainwater is absorbed and thereby inducing/ accelerating the downward movement of rainwater through stem flow and infiltration. On one hand this process creates water bodies like the groundwater reservoirs and rivers, which are good sources of water and nutrients required for plant growth. On the other hand, this process also substantially reduces the soil erosion and the surface flow velocity of storm water. Additionally, there will be release of ample amount of oxygen, generation of colorful and fragrant flowers, fresh leaves as well as fruits through the process of photosynthesis. This makes the entire watershed very pleasant for human beings, migratory birds, flying insects as well as all other animals. The fruits and leaves also serve as food for human beings and animals. A watershed containing large amounts of vegetation is considered as a healthy watershed. It is also called a well-managed or a 'green watershed'. It has no or very limited soil erosion and also it has large reserves of groundwater as well as surface water. In general, it has most of its natural resources conserved. Thus, the scope of watershed management involves all the actions and programs aimed at achieving an overall balance between utilization and conservation of natural resources in a watershed. It represents a sustainable approach for resource conservation through watershed management. In the next section, the Indian and global perspective to watershed management is discussed.

WATERSHED MANAGEMENT

Watershed management is the process of guiding and organizing use of land and other resources in the watershed to provide desired goods and services without adversely affecting soil, water and other natural resources. Watershed management in the broader sense means maintaining the equilibrium between elements of natural eco-system or vegetation, land or water on the one hand and human activities on the other hand. The watershed management programmes aim at improving soil health, soil tilth and drainage and achieving efficient use of harvested and stored rainwater for supplemental irrigation and consequently enhanced productivity and higher economic returns. From community development point of view, watershed management programmes aim at controlling flooding, water logging and soil erosion in order to increase agricultural productivity and a more dependable, cleaner water supply for domestic and industrial use. These programmes also help in minimizing risk of floods in rural and urban areas down streams, reducing sedimentation and conserving natural resources efficiently and effectively. Watershed management programmes strive to improve the lot of the entire farming communities rather than focusing on individual farmers only.

Need of Watershed Management

Watershed degradation in the third world countries threatens the livelihood of millions of people and seriously affects the development of a healthy agricultural and natural resource base. The existing natural resource base is fast depleting due to excessive use of the soil and vegetation system by growing livestock and human population. The population growth exerts pressure on forests, community lands and marginal agricultural lands resulting in inappropriate cultivation practices, forest depletion and grazing intensities. They cause serious damage to the environment by excessive sedimentation of river system affecting the stream flow to downstream users. Watershed management has an important role to play in combating the Malthusian Effect which states that that population tends to increase faster than the means to feed it. Watershed management programmes play an important role in minimizing the Malthusian Effect by ecological and economic rehabilitation of misused watershed slopes, revival of natural streams and augmentation of water resources with active support and participation of people. The watershed management programmes involve the entire community and natural resources particularly land and water resources. Through watershed development programmes, the influence of above factors needs to be observed as given below:

- Socio-economic trend in income generation, employment pattern, household assets, health care education, energy use and impact on women and the landless.
- Perceptions, attitudes and behavior of the people towards project activities and their participation in planning and execution of project and management of resource proposed to be developed under the project together with constraints.
- Productivity/production of crops and forage, changes in cropping pattern and land use adoption or improved cropping practices. Survival and growth of perennial crops on non-arable lands, increase wood and non-wood products and improve livestock milk production.
- Improvement of environment by buildup of vegetative cover, reduction of runoff and soil loss, improvement in livestock milk production policy.
- Use of land and water in vegetation, animal and environment.
- Soil erosion, moderation of floods, alleviation of drought, water availability in soil on surface and underground storage, availability of fuel, fodder and food.
- Development of institutions for planning and implementation.

Focus of Watershed Management
Watershed programmes focus mainly on the following:

- Village common lands as well as private lands; Institutionalized community participation;
- Sustainable rural livelihood support system;
- Decentralized planning and decision making;
- Ridge to valley treatment approach;
- Integrated and holistic development of the watershed unit;
- Protecting natural resources through stakeholders' participation;
- Providing best unit for planning a development programme.

Concept of Watershed Management

Watershed management is based on the concept of sustainability and meeting the needs of present population without compromising the interests of future generation. The concept of watershed management is important for the efficient utilization of water and other natural resources. The concept of watershed management may be expressed in symbolic form by "POWER".

P = Production of food-fodder fuel fruit fibers fish-milk-combine on a sustainable basis.

= Pollution control.

= Prevention of floods.

o = Over exploitation of resources to be minimized by controlling excessive Biotic interferences like over grazing.

= Operational practicability of all on-farm operations and follow up programmes including easy access to different locations in watershed.

W = Water storage at convenient locations for different purposes.

= Wild animal and indigenous plant life conservation at selected places.

E = Erosion control

= Eco-system safety

= Economic stability

= Employment generation

R = Rainwater harvesting

= Recharge of groundwater

= Reduction of drought hazard

= Reduction of siltation in multipurpose reservoirs

= Recreation

POWER is not only important symbolically but watershed programmes bestow real power to the beneficiaries by improving their socio-economic lot.

Problems and Constraints in Watershed Management

A. Land degradation in rain fed areas due to soil erosion from runoff is one of the major problems. In India it was estimated that the soil erosion in the 1990s was almost double that of soil erosion in the 1980s. Rainfall uncertainty and poor economic conditions act as a major constraint and thus prevents the farmers in rain fed areas from making investments. This leads to improper watershed management.

B. Equitable benefit sharing of watershed management within the farming communities as well as within the different locations of watershed is a huge problem. Generally, women, marginal farmers and landless laborers gain very little or nothing at all from the watershed management activities. Several case studies in water scarce states of Gujarat and Madhya Pradesh in India have showed that overdevelopment of water harvesting structures in the upstream portion of watersheds had significantly reduced the inflows into the downstream reservoirs. On the other hand, it is also noticed that building of large reservoirs resulted in the submergence and hardship in the upstream parts and benefits for people in the downstream parts of the same watershed or a neighboring watershed generally having an urban or an industrial area.

C. Acute shortage of water in general and drinking water especially in summer has been observed in many watersheds with inadequate watershed management which may result in severe/ recurrent droughts. It may often result in limited and temporary food productivity gains.

D. Many a times, common lands do not get treated adequately and re-vegetation does not take place as expected in spite of the watershed management programs. As a result of this, domestic/ ecosystem water needs and livestock water/ fodder needs are either inadequately addressed or are made to suffer due to increased water withdrawals by other uses or due to overgrazing.

E. Problems exist or new problems crop up due to improper understanding of the interaction between biophysical and socio-economic processes in watershed management.

F. Conflict among various government ministries such as those related to agriculture [with emphasis on food production], rural development [with emphasis on employment generation & poverty alleviation], forests [with emphasis on maintaining biodiversity & wildlife], as well as conflict between government bureaucracy and elected representatives in their zeal to control funds, is a major problem in watershed management programs -which requires to be resolved on a priority basis.

G. It is hard to conduct meaningful impact assessment studies on watershed management programs for lack of baseline data for monitoring and comparison of the current conditions. The whole exercise of watershed management is undertaken without properly estimating the water supply scenarios under drought/ normal/ surplus years as well as without proper demand management especially during drought years.

H. Large areas inhabited with tribal population lack facilities to harvest water and to stabilize their food/ crop/ fodder production due to reduced forest yields, deterioration in land quality, lack of tribal agriculture policy and population pressure. This leads to a sustained misery, socio-political unrest and insurgency among the tribal population.

New Prospects and Opportunities Associated with Watershed Management

In spite of the above-mentioned problems and constraints as well as some other problems and constraints, watershed management is associated with new prospects and opportunities. Some of them are listed below:

A. There is a need to produce more and better food without further undermining the environment/ ecology, especially the land, water, forests, wildlife and atmosphere. This may include adoption of best management practices (BMPs) such as organic farming, de-silting for reservoir capacity restoration as well as for crop productivity increase, sprinkler and/ or drip irrigation to avoid excess use of water, no tree felling policy, afforestation and arboriculture through high oxygen yielding & other medicinal plants etc.

B. There is a need to ensure that gains due to groundwater recharge are not dissipated by excess groundwater extraction. To achieve this, groundwater over-extraction should be avoided through public awareness and also through regulation.

C. There is a need to consider the downstream impacts of intensive upstream water conservation. For this, watershed associations with representations from all the stakeholders in the watershed should be made operational. These associations can take decisions in the best interest of all the people concerned.

D. Decreasing the costs at which the gains are achieved and thereby increasing the modest benefit-cost ratio should offer new prospect and opportunity in watershed management. To realize this, low cost technologies which may involve local materials, labour at practically no cost, technologies which are traditional and time tested should be employed to generate more benefits spread over the entire watershed among all the stakeholders.

E. Increasing all sections of people's participation beyond the project implementation stage to ensure sustainable watershed management should be a top priority. Only this can ensure progress on a sustained basis overcoming the hydro-geological, socio-political and other uncertainties.

F. Many successful watershed management programs -especially in India, have been implemented on a small scale in a few villages by collaborated efforts among the government departments, non-governmental organizations (NGOs) and research organizations. They represent sporadic BMPs. Hence there is a need to scale up the watershed management activities over large areas which could include remote and/or difficult terrains, so that many problems affecting our agricultural, rural and forest sectors can be effectively addressed.

G. Since there have been no or very few institutions built for research & development on collective management of watersheds, there is a need to build centers of advanced learning employing the modern tools of remote sensing, geographic information systems, decision support systems, computer based planning tools, poverty & socio-economic analysis etc.

H. There is a need to preserve and improve common pool resources (CPRs) of land, water, fodder, forest, fisheries, wild life and agriculture which significantly contribute towards people's livelihood especially in the rural areas.

A. There is a need to minimize migration to urban areas by creating opportunities in agriculture, natural disasters like floods/ droughts, forest/ mountain economies and by arresting fall in agricultural prices, gap in urban/ rural wages, gaps in urban/ rural employment opportunities.

Watershed Management Approaches
Integrated Approach

This approach suggest the integration of technologies within the natural boundaries of a drainage area for optimum development of land, water, and plant resources to meet the basic needs of people and animals in a sustainable manner. This approach aims to improve the standard of living of common people by increasing his earning capacity by o/erring all facilities required for optimum production. In order to achieve its objective, integrated watershed management suggests to adopt land and water conservation practices, water harvesting in ponds and recharging of groundwater for increasing water resources potential and stress on crop diversi1cation, use of improved variety of seeds, integrated nutrient management and integrated pest management practices, etc.

Consortium Approach

Consortium approach emphasizes on collective action and community participation including of primary stakeholders, government and non-government organizations, and other institutions. Watershed management requires multidisciplinary skills and competencies. Easy access and timely advice to farmers are important drivers for the observed impressive impacts in the watershed. These lead to enhance awareness of the farmers and their ability to consult with the right people when problems arise. It requires multidisciplinary pro1ciency in 1eld of engineering, agronomy, forestry, horticulture, animal husbandry, entomology, social science, economics and marketing. It is not always possible to get all the required support and skills-set in one organization. Thus, consortium approach brings together the expertise of di/erent areas to expand the e/activeness' of the various watershed initiatives and interventions.

Focus and Principles of Water Shed Management

Watershed degradation in the third world countries threatens the livelihood of millions of people and constrains the ability of countries to develop a healthy agricultural and natural resource base. Increasing populations of people and livestock are rapidly depleting the existing natural resource base because the soil and vegetation system cannot support the present level of use. In a sense, the carrying capacity of these lands is being exceeded. As the population continues to rise, the pressure on forests, community lands and marginal agricultural lands leads to inappropriate cultivation practices, forest removal and grazing intensities that leave a barren environment yielding unwanted sediment and damaging streamflow to downstream communities

The focus of watershed development:

- Village common lands as well as private lands
- Institutionalized community participation
- Sustainable rural livelihood support system
- Capacity building
- Decentralized planning and decision-making
- Ridge to valley treatment approach
- Integrated and holistic development of the unit
- Protecting natural resources through stakeholders' participation
- Provides best unit for planning a development programme
- Principles of Watershed Management

The main principles of watershed management are:

- Utilizing land according to its capacity.
- Putting adequate vegetal cover on the soil.
- Conserving as much rainwater as possible at the place where it falls both at farmlands and common property resources: In-situ conservation.
- Draining out excess water with a safe velocity and diverting it to storage ponds and storing it for future use.
- Avoiding gully formation and putting checks at suitable intervals to control soil erosion and recharge ground water.
- Maximizing productivity per unit of area, per unit of time, and per unit of water.
- Increasing cropping intensity and land equivalent ratio through intercropping and sequence cropping.
- Safe productive utilization of marginal lands through alternate land use system.
- Ensuring sustainability of the eco-systems benefiting the man-animal-plant-land-water-complex in the watershed.
- Maximizing the combined income from the interrelated and dynamic crop-livestock-tree-labour-complex over the years.

Limitations of Water Shed Management

- Limited success of watershed programme indicates that it was mainly due to:
- Inadequate analysis of physical and socio-economic environment;
- Indifference to farmers' circumstances;
- Strong bias towards crop production;
- Lack of farmers' involvement; and no flexibility in the technological options to suit farmers' needs and their resources.
- Lack of continuation of the soil and water conservation measures up to the point of financial support;

- Poor acceptance of contour-based water conservation measures due to their disregard to ownership boundaries;
- Antipathy of farmers to maintain structures like diversion drains, which cost money and resources to some farmers but benefited others;
- Inadequate arrangement on social fencing to protect forestry and pasture lands;
- Lack of focus to address the problems of livelihoods of landless laborers;
- Disregard to indigenously known and practiced methods of soil and water conservation; and
- Lack of clear arrangements and understanding on sharing of the harvested water.

Water Shed Management Process

The collection, inventorization and documentation of the resources required for water shed management is known as benchmark survey. The benchmark survey on one hand provides requisite information for suitable watershed planning and on the other hand helps in estimating the effect of watershed management works through evaluation and monitoring. The various resources can be collected, inventoried and documented through the following surveys.

1. **Demographic Survey**

The demographic survey consists of documentation of human and cattle population, wild animals, etc. for better planning. Our basic aim for the development of the watershed is to develop the socio-economic condition of the habitant of the area, hence the related information on these aspects is very necessary.

1. **Vegetation**

The information on type of vegetation, its status, present yield, agronomical practices, etc. helps in identifying the gaps with respect to expected optimum, that is, sustained production. The gap in present and optimum yield of all the vegetation is very important to identify proper control measures.

3. Soil-cum-Land Capability Survey

The information on soil (both chemical and physical properties) including geology, drainage, etc. coupled with topographical and hydrological survey helps in preparation of land capability classification map of the watershed which is the of top sheet, revenue map and other suitable instruments/equipments.

4. Engineering-cum-Topographical Survey

The topographical survey basically consists of demarcation of hillocks, ridges, valleys, depressions, streams, land slope (both degree and length), etc. in order to know the extent of degreeof risk and ease of planning. The engineering survey consists of mapping the existing structural measures of erosion control in the watershed viz. dams, culvert, retaining walls, terracing, bonding, trenching, water harvesting structure, etc. It also provides the opportunity for identification of problem area

Hydrological and Water Resources

This basically helps in estimating the water balance of the watershed for crop production. The information on precipitation and other agro climate logical parameter is generally collected from the meteorological observatory already existing in the watershed or from the nearby area. The information on existing water resources, that is, water bodies, viz. reservoirs, ponds, lakes, wells (both shallow and deep), stream flow, etc. is collected by surveying the watershed.

Now as on today, the thrust has shifted from Watershed Management to Integrated Watershed Management.

The emerging issues or new paradigms of Integrated Watershed Management are:

A. Participation

B. Equality (gender issue, legal issues and policies, landless economically weaker section)
C. Equitability
D. Common property resources
E. Societies, associations
F. Employment generation
G. After care and maintenance
H. Responsibilities
A. Monitoring and evaluation

- Crop yield
- Cropping intensity
- Cropping sequence and rotation
- Ground water level
- Water resources
- Flora and fauna
- Land development index
- Low flow index
- Fertilizer intake index
- Micro-climate
- Runoff and soil loss

J. Partial area concepts

CHAPTER TWO

Characteristics of watershed

- Delineation of Watershed
- Characteristics: Size , Shape , Physiography , Climate, Drainage, Land use, Vegetation, Geology and Soils, Hydrology, Socioeconomics
-

Concept of Topographic or Contour Map

A topographic map is a two-dimensional representation of a portion of the three-dimensional surface of the earth. Topography is the shape of the land surface, and topographic maps exist to represent the land surface.

A Typical Contour Map.

Cartographers solve the problem of representing the three-dimensional land surface on a flat piece of paper by using contour lines, thus horizontal distances and vertical elevations can both be measured from a topographic map.

The terms used to indicate what information is contained on a topographic map are given below:

Map Scale: Maps come in a variety of scales, covering areas ranging from the entire earth to a city block (or less).

Vertical Scale (Contour Interval): All maps have a horizontal scale. Topographic maps also have a vertical scale to allow the determination of a point in three dimensional spaces.

Contour Lines: Contour lines are used to determine elevations and are lines on a map that are produced from connecting points of equal elevation (elevation refers to height in feet, or meters above sea level). The following are general characteristics of contour lines:

- Contour lines do not cross each other, divide or split.
- Closely spaced contour lines represent steep slopes, conversely, contour lines that are spaced far apart represent gentle slopes.
- Contour lines trend up valleys and form a "V" or a "U" where they cross a stream.

- Contour lines cannot merge or cross one another on the map, except in the case of an overhanging cliff.
- Contour lines cannot end anywhere, but close on themselves either within or outside the limits of the map.

On most topographic maps, index contour lines are generally darker and are marked with their elevations. Lighter contour lines do not have elevations, but can be determined by counting up or down from the nearest index contour line and multiplying by the contour interval. The contour interval is stated on every topographic map and is usually located below the scale.

Watershed Boundary Delineation from Contour/Topographic Maps

Topographic maps; for example, have a scale of 1:24,000 (which means that one inch measured on the map represents 24,000 inches (2000 feet) on the ground). They also have contour lines that are usually shown in increments of ten or twenty feet. Contour lines represent lines of equal elevation, which typically is expressed in terms of feet above mean sea level. As you imagine water flowing downhill, imagine it crossing the contour lines perpendicularly.

Watershed Boundary Delineation from Contour/Topographic Maps

The water flow is perpendicular to contour lines. In the case of the isolated hill, water flows down on all sides of the hill. Water flows from the top of the saddle or ridge, down each side as the water continues downhill, it flows into progressively larger watercourses and ultimately into the ocean. Any point on a watercourse can be used to define a watershed.

As one proceeds upstream, successively higher and higher contour lines first parallel then cross the stream. This is because the floor of a river valley rises as you go upstream. Likewise the valley slopes upward on each side of the stream. A general rule of thumb is that topographic lines always point upstream. the direction of stream flow is from point A to point B. ultimately, the highest point upstream is obtained. This is the head of the watershed, beyond which the land slopes away into another watershed. At each point on the stream the land slopes up on each side to some high point then down into another watershed. Join all of these high points around the stream to have the watershed boundary. (High points are generally hill tops, ridge lines, or saddles)

Geographic Information System (GIS) for Watershed Delineation

Aquatic resource managers increasingly require information about the characteristics of watersheds that drain to stream reaches of interest. Furthermore, they need this information for multiple watersheds within states or larger regions. Geographic information systems (GIS), coupled with increased spatial data availability, allow researchers to obtain this information. Information obtained from a GIS-based watershed analysis can include data such as watershed area, watershed climate statistics, soil/geology types, topographic statistics, hydrology, and land use.

Accuracy in Watershed Delineation

Spatial Data Accuracy

Do we simply get better results when using finer resolution source data e.g. DEM? At first, it may seem so, but consider high-resolution (let's say 1m) LiDAR derived DEM. If we have a big road crossing a river in our watershed, it may appear as an elevated surface high enough to change watershed delineation result. Therefore it is sometimes necessary to burn-in existing streams. This process alters DEM such that no bumps on the river appear. While this feature is missing in Spatial Analyst/Hydrology tool, one can find it in more specialized hydrology extensions for GIS like Arc Hydro and Tau DEM.

Raster Data Resampling

During the work with GIS, one will often have to re-project the data in different coordinate systems. To get rid of unnecessary details in case when all other data has much lower resolution and excessive details just take space or vice versa, one may have just a single raster file with no-so-good resolution and certain GIS extension/plug-in would require equalizing spatial resolution. In all these procedures re-sampling is involved. That is interpolation of existing data. There are several re-sampling techniques available in most GIS. One should be aware of what kind of data is dealt with. If it is a land use data, that is when each grid cell is assigned an integer code, the new intermediate cells may be filled using nearest neighbor approach instead of calculating some average. However it is vice versa in case of DEM. One may not want to interpolate the DEM using nearest neighbor approach which is usually default but linear or cubic could become good choices. Unless categorical data (like land use) is used, make sure of using real values and not integers and apply smooth re-sampling.

Objectives of Watershed Management

- The different objectives of watershed management programs are:
- To control damaging runoff and degradation and thereby conservation of soil and water.
- To manage and utilize the runoff water for useful purpose.
- To protect, conserve and improve the land of watershed for more efficient and sustained production.
- To protect and enhance the water resource originating in the watershed.
- To check soil erosion and to reduce the effect of sediment yield in the watershed.
- To rehabilitate the deteriorating lands.
- To moderate the floods peaks at downstream areas.
- To increase infiltration of rainwater.
- To improve and increase the production of timbers, fodder and livestock resources.
- To enhance the ground water recharge, wherever applicable.

Effect of Physical Properties on Watershed Management

Certain physical properties of watersheds significantly affect the characteristics of runoff and as such are of great interest in hydrologic analyses. The effects of each physical property on watershed management are described under the following contents.

Size

The size of the watershed has significant effect on its function. Size of watershed determines the quantity of rainfall received retained and disposed off (runoff). A small watershed is pronounced by overland flow which is main contributor to result a peak flow. While a large watershed has no overland flow significantly, but channel flow is the main characteristic. Large watersheds are also affected by basin storage. Watershed size plays a role here, as it interacts with the extent of land use changes, as well as factors that affect weather and climate. In smaller watersheds, the predominant interaction is between weather scale runoff-causing events and the storm hydrograph; whereas, in larger watersheds, the predominant interaction is between climate-scale runoff-causing events and the annual hydrograph. While large-scale events or land use changes may impact small watersheds and even the storm hydrograph in large watersheds, smaller, localized runoff-causing events tend to produce more intensive precipitation over restricted areas, thus having a greater impact on the storm hydrograph in small watersheds or on small tributaries to larger watersheds.

Shape

The common watershed may be of square, rectangular, oval, fern leaf shaped, polygon-shaped, circular or triangular type and long or narrow. Larger the watershed, higher is the time of concentration and more water will infiltrate, evaporate or get utilized by the vegetation. Reverse is the situation when watershed is shorter in length as compared to width. The shape of the land, determined by geology and weather, greatly influences drainage patterns. The density of streams and the shape of a watershed, in turn, affect the rate of overland runoff relative to infiltration. A circular watershed would result in runoff from various parts of the watershed reaching the outlet at the same time. An elliptical watershed having the outlet at one end of the major axis and having the same area as the circular watershed would cause the runoff to be spread out over time, thus producing a smaller flood peak than that of the circular watershed.

Topography

Topographic configuration such as slope, length, degree and uniformity of slope affect both disposal of water and soil loss. Time of concentration and infiltration of water are thus a function of degree and length of slope of the watershed.

Drainage

Topography regulates drainage. Drainage density (length of drainage channels per unit area), length, width, depth of main and subsidiary channel, main outlet and its size depend on topography. Drainage pattern affect the time of concentration. A watershed with a high drainage density is characterized by quick response. Further, drainage cross section information is needed to determine the extent of flooding during high flows.

Area of the Watershed

The area of watershed is also known as the drainage area and it is the most important watershed characteristic for hydrologic analysis. It reflects the volume of water that can be generated from a rainfall. Determination of a workable size of watershed area is important for a successful watershed management programme.

Length of Watershed

Conceptually this is the distance traveled by the surface drainage and sometimes more appropriately labeled as hydrologic length. This length is usually referred for computing a time parameter, which is a measure of the travel time of water through a watershed (time of concentration). The watershed length is therefore measured along the principal flow path from the watershed outlet to the basin boundary. Since the channel does not extend up to the basin boundary, it is necessary to extend a line from the end of the channel to the basin boundary.

Slope of Watershed

Watershed slope affects the momentum of runoff. Both watershed and channel slope may be of interest. Watershed slope reflects the rate of change of elevation with respect to distance along the principal flow path. It is usually calculated as the elevation difference between the endpoints of the main flow path divided by the length. The elevation difference may not necessarily be the maximum elevation difference within the watershed since the point of highest elevation may occur along a side boundary of the watershed rather than at the end of the principal flow path. If there is significant variation in the slope along the main flow path, it may be preferable to consider several sub-watersheds and estimate the slope of each sub-watershed.

Effect of Geomorphologic Factors and Associated Processes on Watershed Management

Geological Rocks and Soil: Geological formation and rock types affect extent of water erosion, erodability of channels and hill faces, and finally sediment production. Rocks like shale's, phyllites erode easily whereas igneous rocks do not erode. Physical and chemical properties of soil, specially texture, and structure and soil depth influence disposition of water by way of infiltration, storage and runoff. Soil types influence the rate of water movement (lateral and vertical) in the soil. For example, finely grained soils, such as clays, have very small spaces between soil particles, inhibiting infiltration and thus promoting greater surface runoff. Conversely, coarse soils, such as sands, have larger pore spaces allowing for greater rates of infiltration and reduced runoff. Surface roughness, soil characteristics such as texture, soil structure, soil moisture and hydrologic soil groups also affect the runoff in various ways. For example; Soil properties affect the infiltration capacity. Soil particles are usually classified as clay ($d < 0.002$ mm), silt ($0.002 < d < 0.02$), or sand ($d > 0.02$ mm). A particular soil is a combination of clay, silt, and sand particles. Generally, soils with a significant portion of small particles have low infiltration capacity, whereas sandy soils have high infiltration capacity.

Watershed Processes.

Climate: Climate parameters affect watershed functioning and its manipulation in two ways. Rain provides incoming precipitation temporally and spatially along with its various characteristic like intensity and frequency. The amount of rainfall and these parameters along with temperature, humidity, wind velocity, etc. regulates factors like soil and vegetation. Soil properties reflect the climate of the region. In the same way, the vegetation type of a region depends totally on the climate type.

Land Cover/ Vegetation: Depending upon the type of vegetation and its extent, this factor regulates the functioning of watershed; for eg. Infiltration, water retention, runoff production, erosion, sedimentation etc. Vegetation plays vital roles in the water cycle. It intercepts rainfall, impedes overland flow and promotes infiltration. Vegetation also uses water for growth. All of these factors reduce the quantity of runoff to streams. Vegetation binds and stabilizes soil, thereby reducing the potential for erosion. Vegetation also stabilizes stream banks and provides habitat for aquatic and terrestrial fauna. Vegetation functions to slow runoff and reduce soil compaction, allowing better percolation of rainfall into soils (infiltration) and groundwater recharge, which creates better water storage for summer base flows. In addition, the patterns, sizes, and composition of the vegetation affect reduction of soil erosion. Leaves and branches intercept the falling rain and reduce the effect of raindrop splash. Vegetative litter from dead leaves and branches builds up an organic surface that provides protection of the soil layer. Root systems also help to keep soil material stable from moving down slope.

Land Use: Type of land use, its extent and management are the key factors which affect watershed behavior. Judicious land use by users is of vital importance to watershed management and functioning. Change of land use within the watershed, especially within the variable source area, greatly affects the collection capacity and consequent runoff behavior of the watershed. The extent of land use change over the watershed has effects that are similar to the relationship between areal storm extent and watershed size. If the land use changes are local, then the impact of such changes is especially apparent in the storm hydrograph. The storm hydrograph is dominated by local characteristics. For land use changes that cover larger portions of the watershed, the impacts may also be observed in the annual hydrograph.

Characteristics of Watersheds

A watershed is a basic unit of hydrological behavior. On the land surface, it is a geographical unit in which the hydrological cycle and its components can be analyzed. Usually a watershed is defined as the area that appears, on the basis of topography, to contribute all the water that passes through a given point of a stream. A watershed embraces all its natural and artificial (man-made) features, including its surface and subsurface features, climate and weather patterns, geologic and topographic settings, soils and vegetation characteristics, and land use. A watershed carries water "shed" from the land after rain falls and snow melts. Drop by drop, water is channeled into soils, groundwater, creeks, and streams, making its way to larger rivers and eventually the sea.

A Watershed Illustration

Classification of Watershed

Watersheds can be classified using any measurable characteristics in the area like- size, shape, location, ground water exploitation, and land use. However, the main classification of watershed is discussed broadly on the basis of size and land use. Two watersheds of the same size may behave very differently if they do not have similar land and channel phases. The descriptions of different watershed classifications are as below.

Size – The main implication of watershed size appears in terms of spatial heterogeneity of hydrological processes. The spatial variability of watershed characteristics increases with size, therefore, large watersheds are most heterogeneous. As the watershed size increases, storage increases. Based on size, the watersheds are divided into three classes.

Small Watersheds - < 250 km2

Medium Watersheds - Between 250 to 2500 km2

Large Watersheds - > 2500 km2

Small Watersheds: Small watersheds are those, where the overland flow and land phase are dominant. Channel phase is relatively less conspicuous. The watershed is highly sensitive to high-intensity and short-duration rainfalls.

Medium Watersheds: Being medium in size, the workability in these watersheds are easy due to accessible approach. Rather than size, shape of the watershed plays a dominant role. Overland flow and land phase are prominent.

Large Watersheds: These watersheds are less sensitive to high-intensity-rainfalls of short duration. The channel networks and channel phase are well-developed, and, thus, channel storage is dominant.

Land Use – Land use defines the exploitation (natural and human interactions) characteristics of watersheds which affect the various hydrological processes within the watershed. The watershed classification based on the land use can be given as below.

- Agricultural
- Urban
- Mountainous
- Forest
- Desert
- Coastal or marsh, or

Mixed - a combination of two or more of the previous classifications

Agricultural Watershed: Agricultural watershed is the watershed in which agricultural activities (crop cultivation) is dominant. It experiences perhaps the most dynamically significant land-use change. This usually leads to increased infiltration, increased erosion, and/or decreased runoff. Depression storage is also increased by agricultural operations. When the fields are barren, falling raindrops tend to compact the soil and infiltration is reduced. There is lesser development of streams in agricultural watersheds. The small channels formed by erosion and runoff in the area are obliterated by tillage operations. The soil structure is altered by regular application of organic and/or inorganic manure. This, in turn, leads to changed infiltration characteristics.

Urban Watershed: These are the watershed areas having maximum manipulation for the convenience of human being. These are dominated by buildings, roads, streets, pavements, and parking lots. These features reduce the infiltrating land area and increase imperviousness. As drainage systems are artificially built, the natural pattern of water flow is substantially altered. For a given rainfall event, interception and depression storage can be significant but infiltration is considerably reduced. As a result, there is pronounced increase in runoff and pronounced decrease in soil erosion. Thus, an urban watershed is more vulnerable to flooding if the drainage system is inadequate. Once a watershed is urbanized, its land use is almost fixed and its hydrologic behavior changes due to changes in precipitation.

Mountainous Watershed: Because of higher altitudes, such watersheds receive considerable snowfall. Due to steep gradient and relatively less porous soil, infiltration is less and surface runoff is dominantly high for a given rainfall event. The areas downstream of the mountains are vulnerable to flooding. Due to snow melt, water yield is significant even during spring and summer.

Forest Watershed: These are the watersheds where natural forest cover dominates other land uses. In these watersheds, interception is significant, and evapotranspiration is a dominant component of the hydrologic cycle. The ground is usually littered with leaves, stems, branches, wood, etc. Consequently, when it rains, the water is held by the trees and the ground cover provided greater opportunity to infiltrate. The subsurface flow becomes dominant and there are times when there is little to no surface runoff. Because forests resist flow of overland water, the peak discharge is reduced. Complete deforestation could increase annual water yield by 20 to 40 %.

Desert Watershed: There is little to virtually no vegetation in desert watersheds. The soil is mostly sandy and little annual rainfall occurs. Stream development is minimal. Whenever there is rainfall, most of it is absorbed by the porous soil, some of it evaporates, and the remaining runs off only to be soaked in during its journey. There is limited groundwater recharge due to occurrence of less rainfall in these watersheds.

Coastal Watershed: The watersheds in coastal areas may partly be urban and are in dynamic contact with the sea. Their hydrology is considerably influenced by backwater from wave and tidal action of the sea. Usually, these watersheds receive high rainfall, mostly of cyclonic type, do not have channel control in flow, and are vulnerable to severe local flooding. In these watersheds, the water table is high, and saltwater intrusion threatens the health of coastal aquifers, which usually are a source of the fresh water supply.

Marsh or Wetland Watershed: Such lands are almost flat and are comprised of swamps, marshes, water courses, etc. They have rich wildlife and plenty of vegetation. As water is no limiting factor to satisfy evaporative demand, evaporation is dominant. Rainfall is normally high and infiltration is minimal. Most of the rainfall becomes runoff. The flood hydrograph peaks gradually and lasts for a long time.

Mixed Watershed: These are the watersheds, where multiple land use/land cover exists either because of natural settings or due to a combination of natural and human interaction activities. In these watersheds, a combination of two or more of the previous classifications occurs and none of the single characteristics dominate the area. In India, most of the watersheds are of mixed nature of characteristics, where agriculture, forest, settlements (urban and rural) etc. land use occurs.

Watershed Characteristics: Physical and Geomorphologic Characteristics associated with Watersheds

Watershed geomorphology refers to the study of the characteristics, configuration and evolution of land forms and properties; developing physical characteristics of the watershed. It comprises of the characteristics of land surface as well as the characteristics of the channels within the watershed/basin boundary. These properties of watersheds significantly affect the characteristics of runoff and other hydrological processes. The principal watershed characteristics are:

• Basin Area

- Basin Slope
- Basin Shape
- Basin Length

Basin shape is reflected by a number of watershed parameters as are given below.

- Form Factor
- Shape Factor
- Circularity Ratio
- Elongation Ratio
- Compactness Coefficient

Along with the surface characteristics of a watershed, the channel characteristics are important in transiting the runoff water from the overland region to channels (streams) and also from the channel of one order (primary) to the other higher order (e.g. river stream). The most common and important channel characteristics of the watersheds are:

- Channel Order
- Channel Length
- Channel Slope
- Channel Profile
- Drainage Density

The quantification of these physical and geomorphologic properties of watershed/basin are important for estimating the watershed hydrologic processes.

Quantitative Characteristics of Watersheds

Physical Characteristics

Watershed geomorphology refers to the physical characteristics of the watershed. Basin area, basin length, basin slope, and basin shape are the physical characteristics of watersheds, significantly affecting the characteristics of runoff and other hydrologic processes. The quantification of these watershed/basin characteristics can be done as discussed below.

Basin Area: The area of watershed is also known as the drainage area and it is the most important watershed characteristic for hydrologic analysis. It reflects the volume of water that can be generated from a rainfall. Once the watershed has been delineated, its area can be determined by approximate map methods, planimeter or GIS.

Basin area is defined as the area contained within the vertical projection of the drainage divide on a horizontal plane. Watershed area is comprised of two sub-components; Stream areas and Inter-basin areas. The inter-basin areas are the surface elements contributing flow directly to streams of order higher than 1. Stream areas are those areas that would constitute the area draining to a predetermined point in the stream or outlet. For example, the stream area for first-order streams would be delineated by measuring the drainage area for each first-order channel. Horton (1945) inferred that mean drainage areas of progressively higher orders might form a geometric sequence. This characteristic was formulated as a law of drainage areas.

Where Aw = mean area of basins of order w, A1 = mean area of first-order basins, Ra = Stream Area Ratio and normally varies from

3 to 6

$$Ra = Aw/Aw\text{-}1$$

Basin Length: Length can be defined in more than one way

- The greatest straight-line distance between any two points on the perimeter
- The greatest distance between the outlet and any point on the perimeter
- The length of the main stream from its source (projected to the perimeter) to the outlet

Conceptually the basin length is the distance traveled by the surface drainage and sometimes more appropriately labeled as hydrologic length. This length is generally used in computing a time parameter, which is a measure of the travel time of water through a watershed. The watershed length is therefore measured along the principal flow path from the watershed outlet to the basin boundary. Since the channel does not extend up to the basin boundary, it is necessary to extend a line from the end of the channel to the basin boundary. The measurement follows a path where the greatest volume of water would generally travel.

Basin length, Lb, is the longest dimension of a basin parallel to its principal drainage channel and Basin width can be measured in a direction approximately perpendicular to the length measurement. The relation between mainstream length and drainage-basin area for small watershed is given below; where Lb is in km and A in km2.

$$Lb = 1.312 \, A0.568$$

Basin Slope: Watershed/basin slope affects the momentum of runoff. It reflects the rate of change of elevation with respect to distance along the principal flow path. It is usually calculated as the elevation difference between the endpoints of the main flow path divided by the length. The elevation difference may not necessarily be the maximum elevation difference within the watershed since the point of highest elevation may occur along a side boundary of the watershed rather than at the end of the principal flow path. If there is significant variation in the slope along the main flow path, it may be preferable to consider several sub-watersheds and estimate the slope of each.

Basin slope has a profound effect on the velocity of overland flow, watershed erosion potential, and local wind systems. Basin slope S is defined as

$$S = h/L$$

Where h = fall in meters, and L = horizontal distance (length) over which the fall occurs.

Basin Shape: Basin shape is not usually used directly in hydrologic design methods; however, parameters that reflect basin shape are used occasionally and have a conceptual basis. Watersheds have an infinite variety of shapes, and the shape supposedly reflects the way that runoff will "bunch up" at the outlet. A circular watershed would result in runoff from various parts of the watershed reaching the outlet at the same time. An elliptical watershed having the outlet at one end of the major axis and having the same area as the circular watershed would cause the runoff to be spread out over time, thus producing a smaller flood peak than that of the circular watershed. A number of watershed parameters have been developed to reflect basin shape. Form factor, shape factor, circularity ratio, elongation ratio, and compactness coefficient are the typical parameters; important in defining the shape of a watershed/basin; and are discussed as below.

Form Factor: The area of the basin divided by the square of axial length of the basin; where value < 1

$$A/L2$$

Shape Factor: The drainage area divided by the square of the main channel length; where value > 1

$$L2/A$$

Circularity Ratio: The ratio of basin area to the area of a circle having the same perimeter as the basin; where value £ 1

$$12.57 \ A/Pr2$$

Elongation Ratio: The ratio of the diameter of a circle of the same area as the basin to maximum basin length; where value £ 1

$$1.128A0.5/L$$

Compaction Coefficient: The perimeter of the basin divided by circumference of equivalent circular area; where value [3] 1

$$0.2821Pr/A0.5$$

Channel Characteristics

The basin geomorphology plays an important role in the transition of water from the overland region to channels (streams) and also from the channel of one order to the other. It is easily determined by contour map and drainage map of the basin. Channel order, channel length, channel slope, channel profile, and drainage density are the most common channel characteristics, important in estimating the watershed hydrological processes and are discussed as below.

Channel Order: The first-order streams are defined as those channels that have no tributaries. The junction of two first-order channels form a second-order channel. A third-order channel is formed by the junction of two second-order channels. Thus, a stream of any order has two or more tributaries of the previous lower order. This scheme of stream ordering is referred to as the Horton-Strahler ordering scheme.

The Horton-Strahler ordering scheme.

$$Nw = RbW\text{-}w$$

Or

$$LogNw = W \log Rb \text{ - } w \log Rb = a - b$$
$$(a = W \log Rb, b = w \log Rb)$$

WhereNw = number of streams of order w; W = order of the watershed; and Rb = Bifurcation Ratio varies between 3 and 5. This law is an expression of topological phenomenon, and is a measure of drainage efficiency.

Bifurcation ratio is defined as the ratio between the numbers of streams of a particular order to the number of streams of one higher order.

$$Rb = Nw/Nw+1$$

Channel Length: This refers to the length of channels of each order. The average length of channels of each higher order increases as a geometric sequence. Thus, the first-order channels are the shortest of all the channels and the length increases geometrically as the order increases. This relation is called Horton's law of channel lengths and can be formulated as:

WhereLw = total length of all channels of order w; Nw = number of channels of order w; Lw = mean channel length of order w; L1 = mean length of the first-order streams; RL = Stream-Length Ratio generally varies between 1.5 and 3.5

$$RL = Lw/Lw\text{-}1$$

Channel Slope: The channel slope is determined as the elevation difference between the endpoints of the main channel divided by the channel length.

Channel Profile: It includes the point of origin of the stream called the head, the point of termination called the mouth, and a decreasing gradient of the stream channel towards the mouth.

Drainage Density: Drainage density (Dd) is the measure of closeness of drainage spacing. It is the indication of drainage efficiency of overland flow and the length of overland flow as well as the index of relative proportions. It is defined as the length of drainage per unit area. This term was first introduced by Horton (1932) and is expressed as

$$Dd = L/A$$

or

Where L = Total length of all channels of all orders, A = Area; W = Basin order; Nw = No. of basin of different order.

Horton (1945) recommended using one-half the reciprocal of the drainage density to determine the average length of overland flow (L0) for the entire drainage basin

$$L0 = 1/(2\,Dd)$$

Where Dd basically describes the average distance between streams and L0 approximates the average length of overland flow from the divides of the stream channels.

WATERSHED MANAGEMENT ISSUES

Given the nature of the changes which are likely as a result of climate change, we can expect impacts in virtually all aspects of the strategies and procedures currently in place for managing watersheds. For the sake of clarity, some of the key categories and some of the potential impacts are outlined below.

Flood Control

The climate impacts with regard to flood control will be seen through the change in the hydrologic cycle. A change in meteorological inputs will result in changes within the hydrologic flow regime of a watershed. Typical flooding impacts will result from more severe weather giving more intense rainfalls at an altered frequency of occurrence. Additional changes would be an increased number of mid-winter melts as a consequence of warmer winter temperatures. These changes will have varying impacts on individual watersheds and watercourses. Those watercourses sensitive to thunderstorm type flooding may experience more frequent and extensive flooding problems.

Watersheds which typically are only impacted by spring snow melt flooding may have a reduced flood risk due to mid-winter snow pack losses or may have risks shifted earlier into the winter period. Changes in the melt of snowpack's, such as earlier snowmelt runoff events may also impact other water management issues such as reservoir operations. Similar to the issue of flood impacts, a change in intensities and susceptibility to severe thunderstorm type events will tend to reduce the effectiveness of flood warning.

These intense storms tend to occur with shorter lead times. Our current forecast abilities fall short in terms of accurate timing and rainfall amount prediction. In addition, with the shift to more intense storms, will come the increase in urban flood issues such as storm sewer surcharging, street flooding and basement flooding. In areas with combined storm and sanitary services, overflows may become more commonplace.

The issue of not only more sever and frequent thunderstorm type events may be compounded by the likelihood of more severe and frequent major tropical storms impacting Southern Ontario. With the likelihood of more frequent or severe Hurricane events, it may simply be a matter of time before a storm at or above the magnitude of Hurricane Hazel impacts the Province. While the Province through its

Flood Plain Planning Policy has reduced the impacts of flood damages very effectively, a storm which exceeds current design standards applied would result in significant damages and risk to life within ourwatersheds. Current policies in place to deal with flooding will be impacted. These policies range from design standards for the regulatory flood to the operation of existing structural flood control facilities.

Erosion Control

Watershed Management strategies also have been developed that attempt to mitigate the impacts of urbanization on erosion processes within the basin. Erosion is a natural process related to the fluvial geomorphology of the watercourse. A stable system tends to reflect a balance between erosion anddeposition along the watercourse reaches. As noted previously, urbanization has resulted in changes tothese processes through changes in the flow regime or the flow conveyance system. Additional changesas a result of climate change will tend to create erosion within stable watersheds and further increaseerosion problems within watercourses currently undergoing changes. The low flow channel of a stableriver/stream system reflects the need of the conveyance feature related to the bankfull flow need withinthe watershed. The return period associated with the bankfull, or channel forming flow, is typicallydefined to be at or near the 1.5 year flow rate. Should climate change lead to increases in the frequencyof severe storms and in the frequency of the channel forming flows, it can be expected that our rivers and streams will react to reflect the changes at this flow rate. An additional area of concern related to erosion centres on a potential increase in freeze / thaw along the stream banks as a consequence of a change in mid-winter melt events. An increase in these events will tend to cause structural failures within the banks, further destabilizing them, increasing slumping and erosion.

Storm water Management

Stormwater management reflects a program specifically designed to mitigate impacts related to changes within the hydrologic cycle due to urbanization. This program has also evolved from one related to flood and erosion control to one which attempts to deal with issues of both water quantity and quality. With the impacts expected within our watersheds related to flooding and erosion, this program and the hundreds of facilities developed to mitigate urbanization impacts will also undergo significant impacts. Existing facilities will no longer be in position to provide the levels of quality or quantity control they presently provide, and may in some instances be at risk of failure.

Fisheries Management

Management strategies related to maintaining, enhancing, or developing a sustainable fishery on a watershed basis is one program which directly depends on the flow regime within the basin. The aquatic environment is supported by the base flow within the watercourse, base flow being defined as the input of groundwater flow into the watercourse. The base flow or low flow component of the overall flow regime forms the aquatic habitat which supports the aquatic environment, including fisheries. The likely climate change impacts within the fluvial system will have serious implications on a Watershed's abilities to maintain its current fishery. In addition to these physical impacts, the increase in mean annual temperature will be reflected in the temperature of ground water inputs to the watercourses. Even a small increase in stream flow temperature will result in cold water habitats being lost or seriously degraded. Temperature changes have the potential for a major shift in the type of fisherythat the watershed may be able to support, regardless of any habitat issues.

Terrestrial Management

Watershed Management programs and policies also encompass terrestrial habitats as well as aquatic. Identifying Environmentally Significant features, such as forest blocks, wetlands, valley and stream corridors, and developing policies or procedures to protect and enhance these features is a major component of management strategies. These features contain functions related to the flora and fauna within them, provide a social function for the residents of the watershed, and provide benefits related to the hydrologic cycle.

Changes within the climate will result in significant impacts and changes within these features as well.The increase in temperatures will extend growing seasons and allow for additional plant species to enter the watershed, many of which could very well be invasive and force changes in the existing biodiversity. The changes in temperature may also allow for a movement of additional animal and bird species into the watershed or the movement out of or extinction of existing species. Changes in meteorological inputs such as extended drought periods will also create stress within the flora and fauna, resulting in changes such as population reductions in some species or the eventual replacement with species of flora and fauna more resistant to these types of climate changes.

Adapting Watershed Management to Climate Change

Climate change will affect all aspects of our ecosystem and we lack a great deal of specific information to comprehensively address each individual issue, however the following reflects some areas where adaptation may be required.

Surface Hydrology

Modelling of the surface hydrology within a watershed should be updated to allow for impacts of climate change to be analysed. Models based upon a continuous flow simulation, and based upon a water budget approach, will allow for a series of climate variations and their impacts to be reviewed and sensitivities and trends of potential impacts identified. Once completed, regulatory flood standards will be assessed, revised bankfull flow estimates defined, and strategies developed to address these flow changes. Policies and procedures need to be developed to deal with the changes in the fluvial components of a watercourse, such as erosion, and meander belt movements to allow for revised channel design standards, and remediation. Planning related to impacted infrastructure such as bridges, culverts, sewers, and outfall structures, needs to be addressed. Flood risk planning and remedial works associated with minimizing future flood vulnerabilities can be identified, prioritized, and undertaken as required. Operational viability of existing flood control structures can be assessed, and operationalmodes revised to account for a revised flow regime, as detailed climate change assessments aredeveloped.

Aquatic Environment

Fisheries management plans will be revised and updated to reflect the most effective way of dealing withclimate change impacts through identification of resources which will be sensitive to climate impacts. The management plans will then reflect how these resources could then be protected, enhanced or managed to reflect the long term habitat and species changes.

Terrestrial Environment

Terrestrial natural heritage strategies will include policies and programs which allow both the adaptation of planting, restoration, and management plans to reflect climate change and also to allow for the mitigative aspect of the terrestrial environment as a carbon sink to assist in reducing greenhouse gasses in the atmosphere.

CLIMATE CHANGE SCIENCE NEEDS

To define the impacts of climate change at a level of detail where effective adaptation can beincorporated into Watershed Management, a great deal of additional study and information will be required. Several areas of additional need are:

- A much more defined assessment of climate impacts on a watershed or a regional scale is required to facilitate any form of modelling and assessment.
- Climate projection improvements should be an assessment of storm frequency change as the typical design approach of looking back to plan forward will likely not remain as a functional tool.
- An assessment of major weather events such as hurricanes and their potential impacts on the Province.
- Studies to look at evaporation changes and their potential impacts to lake levels, droughts and the terrestrial environment.

The impacts and resultant changes that are anticipated from climate change on all the natural features and processes presently managed on a watershed basis will be occur over a time frame stretching into the second half of this century. Watershed Management plans are documents which incorporate policies, strategies, and programs designed to manage natural processes over an extended time frame, and as such, provides the ideal platform, and set of tools to allows for adapting to climate change.

History of Watershed Development in India:

The earliest record of water management by manipulating the natural water regime in India is found in Inamgaon near Pune. During the rule of the Mauryan Dynasty (320 BC) the construction of water harvesting structure (WHS) and sustainable irrigated agriculture in semi-arid regions attained a high level of perfection. The golden age of tank construction in the Deccan Plateau was the reign of Chalukyas of Lakyan (973 to 1336 AD). At national level, Soil Conservation Board was established in the Ministry of Food and Agriculture during the first five year plan (1951-56). Under the control of this Board, a chain of Soil Conservation Research, Demonstration and Training centres were established in the latter period of first plan and early period of second plan.

Sr.no

Location

Establishment Date

Problem area covered

1.

Dehra (HQ)
Dun 20th September, 1954
North-western Himalayan Region

1.

Ootacamund
20th October, 1954
Southern hilly high rainfall region

3.

Kota
19th October, 1954
Ravine problem on the banks of Chambal river

4.

Bellary
20th October, 1954
Black soil region (semi-arid)

5.

Vasad
11th May, 1955
Ravine problem on the banks of Mahi river (Gujarat)

6.

Agra
1 st October, 1957
Ravine problem on the banks of Yamuna river

7.

Chandigarh
1 st October, 1957
Sub-mountain tracts in NE region of India (Shiwalik hills)

8.

Ibrahimpatnam
12th October, 1962
Red soil region (semi-arid)

Watershed development (WSD) projects in the country has been sponsored andimplemented by GOI from early 1970s. Various WSD programmes were launchedsubsequently in various hydro-ecological regions which were primarily focused on soil conservation and water harvesting during 1980s and before. The GOI appointed a committee in 1994 under the chairmanship of Prof. C.H. Hanumantha Rao. The committee gave new guidelines for WSD programmes in 1995 and strongly emphasised on collective action and participation of primary stakeholders, local community, NGOs and Panchayati Raj Institutions.Need for unification of multiplicity of watershed development programmes within the framework of a single national initiative was felt in 2001. A sub-committee constituted for this purpose suggested common guidelines for watershed development projects through Nation Authority for Development of Rainfed Areas (NAFDORA). This finally resulted in set up of National Rainfed Area Authority (NRAA) in November, 2006. The Common guidelines for WSD were released in 2008 (called Neeranchal guidelines) and revised in 2011 and 2013.

Chronology of watershed development (WSD) programmes and policies adopted in India are given below:

- 1973-74 : Drought Prone Area Programme (DPAP)
- 1977-78 : Desert Development Programme (DDP)
- 1987 : National Research Centre for Agroforestry, Jhansi
- 1989-90 : Integrated Wasteland Development Programme (IWDP)
- 1989 : Integrated Afforestation and Eco-Development Scheme (IAEPS)
- 1990-91 : National Watershed Development Project for Rainfed Areas (NWDPRA)
- 1992 : Indo-German Watershed Development Programme (IGWDP)
- 1994 : Guidelines for Watershed Development
- 1998 : National Agricultural Technology Project (NATP)
- 1999-2000: Watershed Development Fund
- 2001 : Common Guidelines for Watershed Development (Revised)
- 2002 : National Afforestation Programme
- 2003 : Hariyali Guidelines released
- 2005 : Mahatma Gandhi National Rural Employment Guarantee Scheme (MGNREGS)
- 2006 : Parthasarathy Committee report
- 2006 : National Rainfed Area Authority (NRAA)
- 2008 : Common Guidelines for WSD (called Neeranchal) released

- 2009 : Integrated Watershed Management Programme (IWMP)
- 2011 : Revised Common Guidelines for WSD were released
- 2013 : Revisions added to 2008 Neeranchal Guidelines

• 45 •

CHAPTER THREE

Hydrological process in watershed

- Precipitation, interception, infiltration, evaporation, evapo-transpiration, surface runoff, ground water-flow, water budget
- Hydrological cycle

The Hydrologic Cycle

It refers to the continuous circulation of water within the earth's hydro-sphere. Water moves into and from the various sources on, over and below the earth, with the total mass of water remaining fairly constant. The water cycle is highly crucial to maintain the life on earth, as it replenishes the world's freshwater resources and moderates extremes in climate. The physical processes involved in hydrologic cycle are

- Evaporation
- Condensation
- Sublimation
- Precipitation
- Transpiration,
- Interception,
- Infiltration,
- Percolation
- The runoff

Sun is the source of energy to activate

Evaporation - It involves the vaporization of water from the water sources due to heat energy of solar radiation. The evaporated water gets converted into cloud. Through which water gets fall on the earth system in terms of precipitation. In water transfer process about 90% of atmospheric water is contributed by evaporation.

Condensation- It refers to the transformation of evaporated water vapours into liquid water droplets suspended in the air as clouds or fog. It is important process to convert the evaporated water into liquid state enabling formation of clouds with the aid of condensation nuclei.

Sublimation- This is the process in which there is direct conversion of solid ice into water vapour. By this process water mass is also added to atmosphere for cycling.

Precipitation- It is the fall of atmospheric water to the ground surface. Under this process the water becomes available for its distribution (surface and sub-surface) and circulation on the above and below the earth surface. It mostly takes place in the form of liquid (rainfall) and very little in solid form (snow, sleet, hail fog etc.)

Transpiration- It is a process of water loss from plants' leaves through respiration. The water loss through transpiration and evaporation coupled together is referred to Evapotranspiration (ET). In hydrologic cycle about 10% water or moisture is added to the atmosphere by transpiration process.

Interception- This is the process in which a part of precipitation is abstracted by the objects lying on the ground surface. The objects may be the crop, tree, natural vegetation and any other in live or dead conditions. Intercepted precipitated water is ultimately lost through evaporation process. Rate and quantity of water loss under this process varied with the type and characteristics of vegetation/ objects and climatic condition, mainly.

Infiltration- It is defined as the entry of water into the soil by crossing the imaginary boundary between soil and atmosphere and its rate called infiltration rate. Under this process the precipitated water moves into the soil media and ultimately joins to the water –table or deposited on impervious layer, if there occurs across water movement path. It is treated as the input process for ground water occurrence.

Runoff- The flow of joined rain water in the stream is designated as the channel flow or the runoff. The characteristics associated to the climate and watershed affects the quantum of runoff at the outlet. Runoff is categorised into surface and sub-surface runoff. In which surface runoff is that part of the runoff which travels over the ground surface thought the channels/ streams /rivers to reach the basin outlet, and sub- surface or indirect runoff points to the flow of precipitated water below the soil surface leading to water- table.

The view of hydrologic cycle is presented in

View Hydrologic cycle

Divisions of Hydrology: Hydrology can generally be divided into two main branches engineering

Hydrology: Engineering hydrology deals with the planning, design and Operation of Engineering projects for the control and use of water

Applied Hydrology: Applied hydrology is the study of hydrological cycle, precipitation, runoff, relationship between precipitation and runoff, hydrographs, Flood Routing

Chemical Hydrology: Study of chemical characteristics of water. Eco-hydrology: Interaction between organisms and the hydrological cycle.

Hydrogeology: Also referred to as geo-hydrology, is the study of the presence and movement of ground water.

Hydro-informatics: is the adaptation of information technology to hydrology and water resource applications

Hydrometeorology: It is the study of the transfer of water and energy between land and water body surfaces and the lower atmosphere.

Isotope Hydrology: It is the study of isotropic signatures of water (origin and age of water). Surface

Water Hydrology: It is the study of hydrologic processes that operate at or near earth's surface. Ground Water

Hydrology: It is the study of underground water.

Hydrologic Budget

It consists of inflows, outflows, and storage, presented by the following equation: Inflow = Outflow +/- Changes in Storage Inflows contribute or add water to the different parts of the hydrologic system, outflows remove water from them, and storage is the retention of water by parts of the system. Since, water movement is cyclical; therefore, an inflow for one part of the system is an outflow to another. As example, for an aquifer the percolation of water into the ground is the inflow to the aquifer while discharge of groundwater from the aquifer to a stream is an outflow. Over time, if inflows to the aquifer are greater than its outflows, the amount of water stored in the aquifer will increase. Conversely, if the inflow to the aquifer is less than the outflow, the amount of water stored decreases.

Use of Hydro-meteorological Data in Watershed Planning

Hydro-meteorological data is an important hydrologic data. It includes data on precipitation, abstractions of precipitation and other meteorological parameters which influence the watershed management. Depending on the objectives of watershed planning, the hydro-meteorological data requirement will be different. The watershed planning and management may generally have any one or more of the following objectives along with any one of the following listed features:

Watershed planning objectives and the features associated with them

Sr.no

Watershed planning objective

Associated features

1

Hydrological characterization

Watershed planning

General water balance

2

Flood management and control

Structures [i.e., dams, river training etc.]

Flood forecasting & warning

Flood plain zoning & flood frequency estimation

Coastal inundation

3

Irrigation and drainage

Supply

Demand scheduling

4

Groundwater planning

Recharge

Flooding management

5

Water quality management

Pollution control

Dilution

Salinity & sedimentation management

6

Fisheries and eco-conservation

Hydro-ecology

Hydro-morphology

Watershed planning objective, feature(s) and relevant hydro-meteorological data required

- Hydro-meteorological data requirement
- Precipitation, temperature, humidity, wind speed.
- Precipitation, temperature, humidity, wind speed & direction.
- Precipitation, temperature, evapo-transpiration, synoptic information, forecasts & alerts, medium & long range forecasts.
- Precipitation, temperature, evapo-transpiration, synoptic information.
- Wind speed & direction, synoptic information, forecasts & alerts.
- Precipitation, temperature, humidity, wind speed, medium & long range forecasts.
- Precipitation, temperature, humidity, wind speed, medium & long range forecasts.
- Precipitation, temperature, humidity, wind speed, forecasts & alerts.
- Precipitation, temperature, humidity, wind speed, medium & long range forecasts.

Use of Hydro-Meteorological Data in Hydrological Characterization

The primary concern of a water management agency is with rainfall, river flow and groundwater, and the focus of their activity will be the measurement and analysis of these variables. Historically the main climate variable collected by a water management agency is rainfall, as this, even in the absence of water management or catchment models, will provide an intuitive, subjective or qualitative assessment of the interaction between rainfall, river and groundwater. For the most part, rainfall data are widely available on a daily basis, and can be agglomerated into 10-day, monthly, seasonal values, etc.

The climate data items used are: precipitation, temperature and evaporation, either in conjunction with, or drivers for, hydrological and hydro-geological variables. Evaporation data are produced by measurement using evaporation pans or evaporimeters, or estimated as evapo-transpiration. The most widely used method for the latter is by the Penman-Monteith Equation, which requires measurement of air temperature, humidity (as vapour pressure), solar radiation or duration of sunshine, wind speed and length of day.

The most basic level of providing data for catchment planning is through a "catalogue" approach, where statistics related to locations and areas are presented. However, there are few instances outside of the more developed countries, e.g. USA, Australia, New Zealand, of comprehensive visualization of data-sets. Their establishment requires a lead agency to host the site and have the responsibility for a range of decisions on what the system will provide, including:

- Maintenance of the website
- Regularity of updating
- Content and format of presentation
- Control of access, e.g. user controlled, open public access
- Management of queries.

In the tactical role, a water balance or catchment model needs to be periodically updated on a scale of weeks to consider such requirements as releases for irrigation and power scheduling, and thus the component data has to be regularly updated. Updated data in these applications are often part of a more complex decision support framework, which may involve critical actions outside the immediate brief of the collection agency. The time frame for accessing data may well be at different time intervals than regular processing and publication procedures employed by data collection agencies, which are mostly monthly. The present widespread use of data-logging instruments allows data access and processing to be flexible.

In the operational role data feeds for similar applications as those of a tactical nature may be necessary at short intervals, of a few days or daily. It is more common for water management agencies to collect climate data for their own requirements, than for climate agencies to collect their own hydrological data.

A significant data item in water balance activities is the estimation of evapo-transpiration (ET) as a major component of losses on a range of spatial and temporal scales. Estimation of ET in practical terms has always been a problematic topic. ET requires the measurement of:

- Air Temperature,
- Atmospheric Humidity,
- Radiation Balance,
- Wind Speed,

All of which require integration over a daily period.

Use of Hydro-Meteorological Data in Flood Management and Control

The responsibilities for planning and design of flood management can fall within the brief of planning and infrastructure agencies, whereas operations for major flood defence, which includes such measures as flood forecasting and warning may be the responsibility of water management or meteorological agencies. Catchment management covers dams, diversion structures, and river bank and infrastructure protection.

- **Daily rainfall,**
- **Sub-daily rainfall, at least hourly,**
- **Wind velocity and direction.**

Daily and sometimes sub-daily rainfall are variables collected by both climate and water management agencies, and the greater density of rain gauges in networks used by water management agencies may reduce the need for data from climate agencies.

Wind velocity and direction are most important for dam design, where wind set-up for wave protection is required, but may apply to exposed sections of river embankments. Wind set-up requires information on mean wind speed, duration of winds above certain thresholds, persistent direction and maximum gust velocity.

For flood forecasting and warning, radar measurement of rainfall, weather satellite information, numerical weather prediction and quantitative precipitation forecasting are required. In flood frequency estimation, maximum river levels and discharges are required as part of the extrapolation of the more extreme events. The effects of catchment structure, antecedent conditions and statistical methods may assume that a flood of a given probability is produce by a rainfall of lesser probability. The estimation of probable maximum precipitation (PMP) is a special aspect of flood frequency analysis.

The aim of flood plain zoning is to identify parts of the flood plain, with different categories of risk for planning and development purposes, broadly to define which parts are subject to more frequent flooding. Therefore it has to be avoided for domestic habitation and critical infrastructure.

Coastal flooding, which may also include flooding in estuary areas, can be caused by range of conditions relating to tide, wind speed and direction and atmospheric pressure. Areas showing particular physical structures, including narrowing coastal bays and shelving sea-bed, can be particularly susceptible to a combination of meteorological conditions, defined as a storm surge. The principal observations involved, wind speed and direction, atmospheric pressure and tides, are generally the responsibility of meteorological services, but coastal flood warning operations are often shared between the meteorological and water management agencies.

Use of Hydro-meteorological Data in Irrigation and Drainage

At the highest, strategic, level irrigation and drainage require consideration in terms of long-term national planning, and involve many more bureaucratic operators than just the meteorological and water management agencies. However, as data providers, these two rank in importance alongside the agricultural agency. Tables of daily data are published that include the full range of variables for the calculation of potential evapo-transpiration and a 24-hour measurement of evaporation is included for most stations.

The supply sources for irrigation and drainage can come from surface water and groundwater, and the overall management of these are the responsibility of a water management agency. However, the day-to-day operations will be done by the irrigation managers, based on resource availability, demand and constraints put in place by general water and environmental management. Managing the supply on a small, individual abstraction, or for a major system, requires some information on meteorological forecasts, mostly in the medium term (days and months) and in the longer term, (years or longer) where planning and strategy have to be considered.

Meteorological services could perhaps provide enhanced information for demand scheduling by making available observations from a national or regional network of automatic weather stations (AWS). The latest versions of AWS have sophisticated software for the estimation of evapo-transpiration.

Use of Hydro-meteorological Data in Groundwater Planning

In arid and semi-arid climates, given suitable geological conditions, it can provide the only reliable, large volume source. Its management is a sub-division of the overall brief for water management, and in many countries is done on a departmental basis within the water management agency.

Groundwater is usually characterized by an annual cycle of drawdown and recharge, and its use as a water supply depends on its management within this cycle. There are also cases, due either to the configuration or type of aquifer, or major cyclical climate patterns, e.g. El Nino-La Nina, that cycles over more than one year can occur. Confined aquifers, where recharge is delayed, can show response to rainfall conditions weeks or even months later. Large artesian basins, such as those in the interior eastern areas of Australia and the eastern Sahara, can have responses to seasonal rainfall patterns in peripheral mountains, lagged by several years.

Groundwater recharge takes place during rainy seasons, e.g. monsoon seasons in the tropics, winter in temperate latitudes. When rainy conditions begin to predominate, it is first necessary for the soil moisture deficit (SMD) to be replenished. The magnitude of SMD prior to recharge is a function of evapotranspiration, vegetation and soil type. Groundwater management is done by reference to known trigger levels, which may be particular aquifer water or storage level, or demand criteria.

Groundwater flooding chiefly occurs when aquifer water levels (water table) rise to above ground level, a situation brought about by high rainfall quantities over extended periods. Because of the delayed response in vertical and horizontal flow in aquifers, flooding often takes place sometime after the causative rainfall events, and may persist for some time (days, weeks), as outflow is also controlled by the aquifer characteristics.

Use of Hydro-meteorological Data in Water Quality Management

The catchment management to maintain water quality in rivers, lakes and groundwater is primarily a function of the water management agency. The maintenance of quality is implemented through complex legislation covering chemical, biological and physical characteristics, and a broad range of users, e.g. agriculture, industry, municipalities all have controls under which they must operate. The need for quality maintenance is becoming more stringent, as national and international targets for ecological and conservation measures are put into place.

Incidents of water pollution arise for several reasons, and response to these incidents can often have a dependence on meteorological conditions for their management and restoration of normalcy. A particular issue for the short-term management of sewage is the risk of combined sewer overflows (CSOs). Combined sewers, where foul water and surface water are carried in the same system are widespread in many countries, and when heavy rainfall occurs, rapid surcharge of the system will result in spillage of untreated sewage. It is important for sewer management to be able to identify the types of conditions that cause CSOs.

Dilution is a key method for permitting the discharge of waste which may, even after treatment, still contain some impurities. Depending on the regime of the receiving water, usually a river or a lake, there are obviously advantages to the management and control from a forecast or projection of meteorological conditions, either incidence of rain, or the duration of dry weather. Information on immediate or protracted elevated temperatures is also important, as these can affect the status of the receiving waters.

Problems of salinity and sedimentation are most directly the result of droughts, and in markedly seasonal climates are of greater or lesser significance in most dry seasons. Thus meteorological information on the extent of dry conditions is of considerable importance. Salinity build up in the soils of irrigated areas results from excessive evaporation from water in the top surface of the soil, which brings up salts that have been previously leached, oftenby over-application of water, or maintaining drainage water levels to high.

Use of Hydro-meteorological Data for Fisheries and Eco-Conservation

Fisheries within rivers and lakes are highly dependent on the maintenance of the required water quality to support the whole of the aquatic environment. The hydro-meteorological information requirements for temperature monitoring and drought forecasting are equally relevant here. In addition, high temperatures can be critical for some fishes. In combination with water quality especially under low flow conditions, they can produce stress or death of fish stocks.

Conservation is a very complex topic, and in the water sector concerns complex physical and biological relationships in water-bodies and wetlands. Water management may be affected by catchment-wide initiatives, or by site-specific interventions. Conservation agencies can operate on a range of levels, from international bodies such IUCN (the International Union for the

Conservation of Nature), WWF (World Wildlife Fund), to national and local conservation bodies. These two organizations have become increasingly involved in decision-making on water resources on several levels.

Use of Physiographical Data in Watershed Planning

Physiographical data broadly includes topographic data, land use-land cover data and soil data. In this section, we shall discuss its utility in watershed planning.

Utility of Topographical Data in Watershed Planning

Topographical data involves data on physical/ natural features of the watershed, watershed boundaries, floodplains in the watershed, wetlands and water bodies etc. Depending upon the purpose and the features of watershed planning as listed in Table 8.1, the utility of the topographical data will vary. In many cases, the data on either the spatial variation or the spatio-temporal variation of the topographical data parameters listed below are required.

For hydrological characterization, the data on slope, permeability of the ground surface, roughness of the ground surface, obstructions like buildings or other manmade infrastructure or hills or depressions is required. For flood management and control, the data on wetlands and water bodies, channel cross sections, other natural and artificial flood mitigation structures is required. For irrigation and drainage, data on optimum water table depth, canal linings, canal flow capacity, crop type, crop area are necessary.

For groundwater management, the data on annual changes in water table depth, crop root zone depths, wetlands and water bodies is needed. For water quality management, the locations of point and non-point pollution sources, total maximum daily loads (TMDLs), spatio-temporal variations in pH, turbidity, total suspended solids, total dissolved solids, biochemical oxygen demand (BOD) etc. may be needed. For fisheries and eco-conservation, the data on dissolved oxygen, spatio-temporal variations in aquatic plants and animals having eco-conservation capabilities is required.

Utility of Land Use/ Land Cover (LULC) Data in Watershed Planning

LULC data consists of data on forests, grass/ range lands, cultivated lands, orchards, wildlife reservations, recreation areas, urban/ rural areas, water bodies, eroded areas etc. Depending upon the purpose and the features of watershed planning as listed in Table 8.1, the utility of the LULC data in watershed planning varies. In most of the cases, the data on either the spatial variation or the spatio-temporal variation of the LULC data is required to carry out watershed planning.

LULC influences practically all the processes of hydrologic cycle like interception, infiltration, surface runoff, surface storage, groundwater runoff, groundwater storage, evapo-transpiration (ET). LULC also influences meteorological parameters such as temperature, humidity and wind velocity, which in turn impact the estimation of ET. Therefore especially the purposes of watershed planning like hydrological characterization, flood management and control, groundwater planning in a watershed get affected significantly. Thus LULC data has a great utility in watershed planning.

An improved model performance plays a vital role in achieving the watershed planning objectives. Hence, appropriate values of the lumped and/or distributed model parameters need to be assigned in the model, based on the accurate analysis by experts of the spatio-temporal variations in the watershed LULC data.

Utility of Soil Data in Watershed Planning

Soil data can be an important factor in determining the amount of erosion and storm water runoff that occurs in the watershed of interest. It can enable the estimation of water retained within the soil, analyze the slope stability or the flow of groundwater through the soil pores. Data on the types of soils in the watershed and their characteristics helps us to identify the areas that are prone to erosion or sedimentation as well as the areas which are more likely to experience runoff.

Hydrologic Design as Applied to Recharge Structures

There are three main methods of artificial groundwater recharge as listed below.

- Direct methods.
- Indirect methods.
- Incidental methods.

(A) Direct Methods: Direct methods of recharge can further be subdivided into two main categories as surface methods and sub-surface methods.

(B) Surface Methods: In this method of recharge, water is applied on the permeable ground surface wherein it infiltrates into the unsaturated zone to reach slowly the underground water table. Surface techniques, especially spreading techniques of artificial recharge are most widely used because of their economy and easiness in operation. Various types of spreading techniques are as follows:

- Recharge basins
- Furrows and ditches
- Regulated stream channels

(C) Recharge Basins:

Excavation or building dikes or levees constitute basins [Refer to Fig 13.1]. The shape and size of the basin depends upon topography and availability of land. To reduce deposition of sediments, the water released to the basin should have minimum sediment. This can be achieved by the following measures:

- By water diversion to the basin during the non-flood periods, when the suspended sediment is low;
- By adding certain chemicals in the water to remove sediments;
- By providing Sedimentation basins to hold water before releasing it into the recharge basin.

Requirements of Recharge Basin Sites

- Knowledge of surface geology downward in the basin and laterally away from the basin;
- Considerable knowledge of permeable soil in the basin which permits adequate infiltration rate;
- Sufficient knowledge of the unsaturated zone between ground surface and water table.

Furrows and Ditches

This method of recharge is very useful for irregular terrain. Furrows and ditches should be shallow, flat bottomed, and closely spread to obtain maximum water contact area. Gradient of major ditches should be sufficient to carry suspended material through the system so that surface openings are not clogged due to deposition of fine-grained material. The design of furrows and ditches system depends upon the topography and the size of the area. A downstream collecting ditch is necessary to return excess water to the main channel.

Regulated Stream Channels

The objective of this method is to extend the time and area over which water is recharged from a natural influent stream channel. It requires upstream storage facilities to regulate stream flows and to enhance infiltration. The flow rate of water should be such that it should not exceed the absorptive capacity of downstream channels. Different types of stream channel regulations include:

- Widening, leveling or scarifying a stream channel bed;
- Constructing permanent low check dams;
- Constructing temporary low check dams of stream bed materials;
- Constructing L - shaped finger bikes in straight stream channels and L-shaped hook levees in curved stream channels.

Hydraulic Design Applied to Recharge Structures

In this section, we shall discuss the theory of artificial groundwater recharge. It will be followed by a discussion on spreading in shallow/ deep phreatic aquifers

Theory of Artificial Recharge by Spreading

As a variant of induced recharge, the most likely set-up of an artificial recharge scheme consists of a series of spreading ditches and infiltration galleries arranged alternately at equal intervals. For unconfined aquifers which are pervious up to the ground surface, this set-up offers few difficulties. With slight modifications, it may also be applied for artesian aquifers when the confining layer on the top is thin. For confined aquifers covered by thick deposits of less pervious material, recharge must be accomplished by injection wells, having their own problem and possibilities. The simplest construction of parallel spreading ditches and infiltration galleries is shown in, where the coefficients of transmissivity (kH) of the aquifer as well as the maximum allowable drawdown (S0) are determined by the local hydro-geological conditions. The other factors indicated in this figure viz., q0, L and w, must be chosen such that the purposes of the recharge scheme are fulfilled. Of the recharge scheme are fulfilled.

CHAPTER FOUR

Water and soil conservation in watershed

- Water conservation: Nala Bunding, Check dams, Farm ponds, Percolation tanks, Artificial recharge
- Soil conservation- Contour Bunding, Gully plugging, Trench cum mound, Levelling
-

History of Soil Erosion

Although man could realize the ill effects of erosion much later, he has been unconsciously struggling with the problem since farming started. Man constructed bunds around the cropped plots to conserve water and soil. Farming started about 7000 years ago when man began to settle and leave nomadic life. It is reported that the first civilization started in the plains of Mesopotamia located in the valley of Tigris and Euphrates rivers. It gradually developed into the world's best civilization during the time of the Babylonians, Assyrians etc. The downfall of this civilization can be attributed more to the unwise utilization of the fertile land resources rather than the successive invasion by different regimes.

The Nile Valley consisting of Egypt, Uganda, Sudan and Ethiopia are also considered to be an area of the oldest civilizations of the world. Egypt is called the gift of River Nile. The neighboring countries of Israel, Syria, Jordan, Greece, Turkey etc. were equally prosperous once upon a time. The rainfall being scanty, farmers started irrigation of the crops through canals. Scientific design of canals was unknown to the man and silting started soon. Mesopotamia has been known as the place of the Garden of Eden and the Tower of Babel. There were high density of population and big cities. This land has seen the rise and fall of at least eleven empires. The debris caused due to erosion for centuries left a deep blanket over these big cities and now the ruins of the cities, some scattered villages can be seen here.

Tigris and Euphrates rivers originate from the mountains that have been made devoid of tree cover by felling and flow through overgrazed hill lands. Runoff water that flew from the catchment into these rivers carried huge silt with it. The silt was deposited in the canal below and it was a difficult task to maintain the canal system. With the growth in population, the canal system was further expanded and maintenance became more difficult. Also there has been repeated invasion of the country and it became almost impossible to fight the invaders and to maintain the canals. As a result the canal system and finally the agriculture failed. With a small agricultural production, only a small population could be supported and the great civilization disappeared.

There are innumerable examples of how soil erosion destroyed civilizations. The Jordan River washed off most of the fertile soils from the slopes and bed rocks can be seen there. High lands of Judea have been severely eroded and a very poor yield obtained. The famous Nabatean civilization of about 2000 years ago along with its capital Petra is in ruins now. This can also be attributed to the breakdown of agriculture system due to severe soil erosion. Shanxi, a province of China faced severe soil erosion after the denudation of forests. Many cultivated areas have turned into gullies.

Classic examples of disappearance of human civilization in India due to the mismanagement of soil resources are Mohenjo-Daro and Harappa. Vast tracts of hilly areas of north eastern states have been made barren by jhuming (i.e., shifting cultivation). Siwalik range of the Himalayas suffered a severe soil loss due to denudation and overgrazing by cattle. The eroded soil silted up the river beds. The Kosi River originating from Nepal got silted up due to erosion problems in the upper catchment. Most of the years, it inundates vast areas in North Bihar. River Damodar has been a river of sorrow for the alluvial plains of West Bengal due to erosion problems in Chota Nagpur region of Jharkhand. Again, by construction of reservoirs and treatment of the upper catchment the problem has been largely overcome.

Types of Water Induced Soil Erosion

Soil erosion is broadly classified into natural type called geological erosion and manmade type called accelerated erosion. Geological erosion takes place under natural undisturbed conditions when a balance is maintained between the soil, climate and vegetative cover. It is a very slow process and responsible for soil formation as well as soil loss. Both together maintain a balance for favorable growth of the plants. Most of the present topographical features of the world such as natural channels, valleys, canyons etc. are results of the geological erosion. As far, as agricultural lands are concerned, geological erosion is not of much consequence.

Different activities of man such as cutting of forest, felling of trees, cultivation of land, overgrazing etc. have disturbed the natural balance between the soil, climate and vegetative cover. Under this condition, soil erosion is taking place at a much faster rate and this is called accelerated erosion. It. is destructive in nature and caused much land degradation. Only accelerated erosion is a matter of concern for the agricultural land and henceforth it will be referred to erosion only. The erosion can be classified as:

- **Water Erosion,**
- **Wind Erosion,**
- **Coastal Erosion.**

Depending upon the degree of erosion and its location, water erosion is further classified as:

- **Raindrop Erosion,**
- **Sheet Erosion,**
- **Rill Erosion,**
- **Gully Erosion,**
- **Stream Channel Erosion.**

These are discussed in details in the subsequent sections.

Raindrop Erosion

Raindrop erosion is the result of direct impact of raindrops on bare soil or in thin film of water. If the soil surface is covered with good vegetation, much harmful effects do not occur as the drops break into finer sprays and much of it infiltrates into the ground. However, if the raindrop strikes the bare soil, considerable raindrop erosion takes place. The raindrops sometimes fall at high speed of 50 kmph and the soil particles may be splashed to a height of 60 cm and move laterally to a distance of 150 cm.

The same soil particles are generally splashed more than once. Thus they are detached from the main soil body and easily carried with the runoff water. In a level surface much serious problem may not occur as the soil is just shifted from one place to another. But in sloping lands they are easily transported down the slope and may join a rill or a gully from where further downward movement becomes easier. Apart from soil particles, the plant nutrients are also removed and transported from the productive land.

A part of the rainfall with clay and silt suspension infiltrates into the ground. In this process the fine particles are removed due to sedimentation phenomena. These fine particles block the soil pores and the infiltration capacity of the soil is greatly reduced. As a result, the runoff rate increases and more soil particles are transported. Thus raindrops striking bare soils on sloping ground, causes severe damage which intensifies as the duration increases.

Factors affecting raindrop erosion are (i) vegetative cover and mulches, (ii) rainfall, (iii) wind velocity and direction, (iv) soil texture and structure, (v) topography, particularly degree and length of slope. Raindrops falling on plants, crop residue or other mulches lose their energy before striking the soil. High wind velocity in the direction of slope causes higher splash. The wind velocity and air resistance also affects the raindrop velocity. The raindrop velocity depends upon the height of fall up to a height of about 10.5 m after which it attains the terminal velocity. Soil loss increases with the increase of this terminal velocity which may vary from 4.5 to 9 m/s depending upon the drop size. Surface roughness and obstructions reduce the soil loss due to splashing.

Sheet Erosion

Sheet erosion has been defined as the uniform removal of soil in thin layers from sloping land which results from sheet or overland flow occurring in thin layers. The top fertile layer of the soil is slowly skimmed off every year and it flows down as muddy water. The field appears to be the same as it was before the rainy season. But huge amount of soil gets lost every year. Initially the reduction in the crop yield may not be significant. But over the years the yield declines till it reaches a minimum. Sometimes, the lower layers of soil and finally the bed rock may be exposed rendering the soil unfit for any crop production. Therefore, although sheet erosion occurs slowly but it is very harmful as it cannot be detected easily in the initial stage.

Recent studies on the mechanisms of erosion using remote sensing and other photographic techniques indicate that the type of sheet erosion mentioned above rarely occurs. Along with the detachment and transport of soil particles, the second phase of erosion called rill erosion also takes place. High speed photographs clearly indicate the change of position of the microscopic rills. In case loose topsoil is located above a comparatively light subsoil, combination of sheet and rill erosion easily occurs. For a given soil surface with a fixed size, shape and density of soil particles, the eroding and transporting power of sheet flow is greatly influenced by the depth and velocity of runoff.

Rill Erosion

Rill erosion is called the second erosion in which the removal of soil by rain water from small but well demarcated semi-permanent channels or streamlets takes place due to overland flow. Rill erosion starts simultaneously with sheet erosion. But conventionally rill erosion is said to have started when channels are large enough to be visible.

Like sheet erosion, rill erosion is also often overlooked although detachability and transportability of soil are much higher due to higher surface velocity. If care is taken, channels formed due to rill erosion can easily be smoothed out by farming operations. If proper care is not taken, rill develops both in depth and width. Ultimately movement of small farm implements becomes difficult and cropped area reduces. Finally the rills may develop into gullies.

Gully Erosion

If the rills are not attended for a long time they develop further in their depths and widths and finally form gullies. Gullies are therefore an advanced stage of rill erosion, which is an advanced stage of sheet erosion. Once the gully has been formed, it cannot be smoothed out by normal cultivation practices. It requires costly and effective structures/ practices to control the further advancement of gully.

The advancement of gully depends upon watershed characteristics, rainfall characteristics, soil characteristics, shape of the gully, slope of the channel and cultivation practices in the watershed. Following four different processes are involved in the development of the gully:

- **Waterfall erosion at the gully head**: Water falling at the gully head cuts the edge and caving of banks takes place. This detached mass of soil is carried away by runoff water. If the subsoil is loose, undermining proceeds at a faster rate. The depth and width of the gully thus increase. More land area is covered by gullies and gradually gully branches spread all over the area.
- **Channel erosion**: It is caused by the water flowing through the gully or by raindrop splash on unprotected soil. As much of the water passes through the gully head, lengthening of the gully takes place.
- In cold regions, alternate freezing and melting of snow occurs on the exposed soil banks and causes erosion.
- Due to undercutting, slides or mass movement of the soil takes and huge quantity of soil is lost at a much faster rate.

Generally, the following 4 stages are involved in the development of gullies:

Stage 1: Formation Stage

Channel erosion takes place by downward scour of the topsoil. If the topsoil can provide resistance, this stage proceeds slowly.

Stage 2: Development Stage

Upstream movement of the gully head and simultaneous enlargement of width and depth take place. The weak parent material is rapidly removed.

Stage 3: Healing Stage

Vegetation begins to grow in the channel and further erosion stops.

Stage 4: Stabilization Stage

The gully bed and sides reach a stable slope and sufficient vegetation grows to anchor the soil and to trap soil flowing from upstream. New topsoil develops and vegetative cover grows.

Classification of Gullies: There are several systems of gully classification. According to one system gullies are classified as per their cross-sections. Depending upon soil, climatic conditions, age of the gully and type of erosion it may be either V-shaped or U-shaped. V-shaped gullies are formed due to scouring of soil by concentrated runoff in unprotected depressions. If both the surface and subsurface soil are easily erodible, then U-shaped gullies are formed. Vertical walls are formed due to undermining and collapse of the banks. Both the types of gullies may be visible in the same channel.

Another commonly used method of classification of gullies is based on drainage areas and gully sizes. Based on their works in the ravine lands of Gujarat in 1961, Tejwani and Dhruvanarayana classified gullies into four classes. According to this classification, very small gullies have depths and widths within 3 m and 18 m respectively. Small gullies have depth within 3 m, but width is greater than 18 m and side slopes may be a between 8 to 15 per cent. Medium gullies have depth between 3 to 9 m, bed width 18 m or more. Deep and narrow gullies generally have depths 3 to 9 m and bed width less than 18 m.

Stream Channel Erosion

Stream channel erosion is the removal of soil either from stream bank or from channel bed. The flowing water gradually erodes the river bank(s) or the bed below the water surface. Sometimes, the streams and rivers change their course during the periods of peak flows. This is a very serious problem as the river gets widened every year. The widening of the river destroys huge cultivated lands, villages, cities, railway lines, bridges, other structures etc. Very costly and effective protection measures are required to prevent this type of erosion.

Stream channel erosion consists of two parts namely, bank erosion and scour erosion caused by undercutting. The later is more serious as it can cause huge landslides. The stream bank erosion is caused by removal of vegetation, by overgrazing or by tilling very close to the river bank. The velocity and soil texture etc. influence the scour erosion. Stream channel erosion differs from gully erosion in the following aspects:

- Stream channel erosion occurs at the lower end of the headwater tributaries, whereas, gully erosion occurs near the upper ends of headwater tributaries.
- Stream channel erosion occurs in streams that have almost continuous flow, whereas, gully erosion occurs in streams with intermittent flow.

Measures for Water Induced Soil Erosion Control

Contour Cultivation

Contour cultivation consists of performing all farm operations like ploughing, seeding etc., approximately along contours. Ploughing produces small ridges across the slope. These ridges along with crops arrest themovement of soil and water. In low rainfall areas, contour cultivation helps in moisture conservation. In high rainfall areas, significant amount of soil and a part of water is conserved. The furrows formed due to contour cultivation store large amount of rainwater and allow it more time to infiltrate. Due to uniform soil moisture distribution during entire crop period, the crop yield increases.

Contour cultivation is also an important step in upstream flood control. However, in steep slopes under high rainfall conditions, contour cultivation may cause more harms than benefits. There could be breaking of ridges followed by increased cumulative flow and gully formation. Under such conditions, contour cultivation needs to be supplemented by measures like terracing and bunding. In contour cultivation, gradual surface sealing takes place due to deposition of fine particles and subsequent decrease in infiltration capacity. This should be avoided by suitable desilting measures.

Contour Bunding

Bunding or construction of small embankment is carried out to reduce the length of slope, to reduce the velocity of runoff water and to hold the water in the catchment for a longer period. Thus more water infiltrates into the ground and less run-off and soil erosion take place. Different types of bunds are used for erosion control and moisture conservation.

When the bunds are constructed along the contours with some minor deviation to adapt to practical situations, they are known as contour bunds. If the bunds are constructed with some slope, they are known as graded bunds, Side bunds are constructed along the slope at the two sides of the contour bund. Lateral bunds are constructed along the slope in between two side bunds to reduce the length of the contour bund. This reduces the concentration of runoff water along one side. Supplemental bunds are constructed between two contour bunds to limit the horizontal spacing of the contour bunds. Peripheral bunds are constructed along the field boundaries and may not conform to the contours.

In India, contour bunding or simply bunding has been practiced for a long time and the Indian farmers have very good knowledge about it. First thing that is done to control a rill or a gully is to do bunding. The former state of Bombay did notable works in contour bunding and in other states like Andhra Pradesh, Tamil Nadu and Karnataka vast areas were put under contour bunds. From the experience gained through these constructions, it was known that bunds could stand well only in shallow, medium and medium deep soils. Deep black soils show cracks in dry conditions and the bunds fail. Through these cracks water continues to flow and big breaches are caused. This results in severe damage to the fields. Although various erosion problems exist in black cotton soils, contour bunding cannot be taken up in such soils successfully.

Design of Contour Bunds

The design of contour bund includes determination of spacing, both horizontal and vertical and bund cross-section. The bund cross-section includes base width, side slope and bund height. The bund height should be sufficient to store the expected runoff from a rainfall of 10 years recurrence interval. Over this depth, extra depth should be provided for the design depth of water over the weir and the free board. The base width, side slope and top width are decided by the nature of soil.

Spacing of Contour Bunds

As the water flows through a sloping land, it attains erosive velocity. The bund should be spaced in such a way so as to intercept the erosive velocity. Again, the spacing should not be too close to interfere with the farming operations. Different relationships have been developed for the spacing of bunds.

Soil Conservation Measures

Crops and vegetables which cover the ground surface well and have extensive root system reduce soil erosion. Plant canopy protect the soil from the adverse effect of rainfall. The grasses and legumes produce dense sod which helps in reducing soil erosion. The vegetation provides organic matter to the soil. As a result, the fertility of soil increases and the physical condition of soil is improved.

Following cropping systems help in controlling soil erosion,

Crop rotation: Crop rotation is planned sequence of cropping. Rotation of crop is an important method for checking erosion and maintaining productivity of soil. A good rotation should include densely planted small grain crops, spreading legume crop etc. which may check soil erosion.

Strip Cropping: It consists of growing erosion permitting crop (e.g. Jowar, Bajra, Maize etc.) in alternate strips with erosion checking close growing crops (e.g. grasses, pulses etc.). Strip cropping employs several good farming practices including crop rotation, contour cultivation, proper tillage, stubbles mulching, cover cropping etc. It is very effective and practical means for controlling soil erosion, specially for gently sloping land.

Cultivation of dense plant and grasses: Sod forming crop such as lucern (medicago sativa L), Egyptian Cloveror. Berseem, ground nut (Arachis hypogea L), Sannhemp (Crotolariajuncea), grass etc. cover the surface of the land and their roots bind the soil particles to form soil aggregates, thus preventing soil erosion.

Cultivation of proper crops: Cultivation of row crop in sloppy lands permits soil erosion. In this filed, the crops particularly cereals, fodder crop etc. should be broadcasted and the plants remain haphazardly in field. As a result, the movement of water gets obstacle and more water is absorbed in the soil, thus reducing soil erosion.Mixed and intercropping (CowpeaVigna catjang, with cotton – GossipumSp, maize – Zea mays with soyabean – Glycine max etc.) practice checks the soil erosion and avoids the risks of the crop failure. The land should not be kept without crop: There is very scope of soil erosion if there are no crops on the land. The soil erosion decreases in different way of cropped land.

Afforestation: Afforestation means growing of forests where there were no forests before owing to lack of seed trees or due to adverse factors such as unstable soil, aridity or swampiness. Along with Afforestation, reforestation should be undertaken which means replanting of forests at places where they have been destroyed by uncontrolled forest fires, excessive felling and lopping. Afforestation is the best means to check the soil erosion.

Mulching: Mulches of different kinds such a leaves, straws, paper, stubbles, etc. minimize evaporation and increase the absorption of moisture and protect the surface of the land against the beating action of rain drops. Later on the decay to form humus which improves the physical condition of soil. Natural mulching also helps in the infiltration of water and the reduction of evaporation.

Organic manure: Organic manures improve the soil structure. The crumb and granular structure increases the infiltration and permeability in the soil and conserve the soil water. Consequently soil erosion decreases.

Control of grazing: Grazing increases the soil erosion. But the grazing cannot be completely stopped in all areas. So the restricted and rotational grazing may be helpful in checking soil erosion to some extent. The area open to grazing for sometimes should be closed for the following year to facilitate regeneration of forests and to maintain thick ground vegetation.

Good tillage: Tillage is the mechanical manipulation of soil by different kinds of implements. Tillage makes the soil loose and friable which helps in retention of water. The special method of tillage practices should be followed for the conservation purposes. Tillage may consist of several types of soil manipulation such as ploughing, harrowing, cultivation etc.

Contour bunding: Contour bunding consists of building earthen embankment at intervals across the slope and along the contour line of the field. A series of such bund divide the area into strips and act as barrier to the flow of water. As a result, the amount and velocity of run-off are reduced, resulting reducing the soil erosion. Contour bunding is made on land where the slope is not very steep and the soil is fairly permeable. Contour bunds are also called level terraces, absorbtiontype terraces or ridge type terraces.

Terracing: A terrace is an embankment of ridge of earth constructed across the slope to control run off and to minimize soil erosion. A terrace reduces the length of the hill side slope, thereby reducing sheet and rill erosion and prevents formation of gullies.

There are different types of terraces as follows:

Bench terracing: It consists of transforming relatively steeps land into a series of level or nearly level strips or steeps running across the slope. The soil materials that are excavated from the upper part of the terrace is used in filling the lower part and a small bund is also raised along the outer edge of the terrace to check the downward flow of rainwater and also soil erosion.

Channel terrace: It consists of making of wide but shallow channels across the slope of the land either exactly on contour line or with a slight grade (0.1 to 0.2 per cent). In this process, the excavated soil is placed along the lower edge of the channel in the form of low ridge.

Narrow based terrace: It consists of making a number of narrow based ridges or bunds at a distance of 1m to 2m across the slope of the land at suitable intervals in high rainfall areas.

Broad based ridge terrace: It consists of making wide but low bunds on the contour lines by excavating soils from both sides of terrace. This is practiced in areas where the rainfall is relatively low.

Contour trenching: It consists of making a series of deep pit (i.e. 2ft. wide and 1ft. deep) or trenches across the slope at convenient distance. The soil excavated from the trenches is deposited on the lower edge of the trenches where forest trees are planted.

CHAPTER FIVE

Watershed development

- Application of Remote Sensing and GIS in watershed management
- Integrated watershed development plans
- Importance of watershed management in national development.

Application of Remote Sensing and GIS in watershed management

GIS stands for geographic information system. An information system is a computer program that manages data. A GIS, then, is a type of information system that deals specifically with geographic, or spatial, information. Like other information systems, a GIS requires lots of data that it can access, manipulate, and use to produce a product. Geographic information describes the spatial (location) factors of an object or area. This can be simply latitude and longitude coordinates, but in most cases more complex factors are included. As for a formal definition of GIS, Worboys (1995) define GIS as follows: A geographic information system (GIS) is a computer-based information system that enables capture, modeling, manipulation, retrieval, analysis and presentation of geographically referenced data. The definition provided by The Oak Ridge National Laboratory: GIS is "a digital representation of the landscape of a place (site, region, and planet), structured to support analysis." Under this broad definition, GIS conceivably may include process models and transport models as well as mapping and other spatial functions. The ability to integrate and analyze spatial data is what sets GIS apart from the multitude of graphics, computer-aided design and drafting, and mapping software systems.

The components of a GIS

In order to function properly, a GIS needs several basic components:

Data: organized in a database. The database includes the locational data (where things are located) and the spatial relationships between data features. The database may also include additional relevant information.

Software: a program or group of programs, such as Arc View or Arc/Info, that can access the database, manipulate the data, and produce a product. Others: Idrisi, GRASS, Erdas, etc.

Platform : the hardware, including disk space, terminals, network supporting devices, etc., that support the software and database.

User : people who operate the GIS and use its results for analysis and decision-making The fourth, and final, component of a GIS is the user (this means you!). Without know- ledge able, competent operators, the entire system is useless. Users that are able to creatively employ the functions of the GIS to their fullest extent (not just making maps!) justify the cost and effort required to build and maintain a GIS. The goal of this website is to help you become a competent user, so that you can utilize the power and functionality of GIS products.

Environmental application of GIS

I. Best Management Practices (BMPs) for Nonpoint Source Pollution Control

II. Storm water Management

III. Watershed Management

IV. Spill Control Planning & Response

V. Hazardous Material Management

VI. Air Pollution Management & Planning

VII. Wetlands Delineation

VIII. Forestry Management
 IX. Mining & Geologic Resource Management
  X. Wildlife Habitat Management

Some software in watershed management MMS Modular Modeling System (PRMS, TOPMODEL)

Weasel The GIS Weasel (PRMS and TOPMODEL interface)

HSPF Hydrological Simulation Program—Fortran

PRMS Precipitation-Runoff Modeling System

We all have ideas about the state and history of the watershed and about how that watershed will respond to alternative land management plans. Our personal ideas are models of the world around us. These models are used to help us understand the present and predict the future. Often each of us has different views of the present and the future and we find it very difficult to communicate why in a particular set of future consequences. To help this communication, it may become necessary to formalize those views and ideas for better communication between us. Geographic information systems (GIS) allow us to formally define our understanding of the past and present state of our watershed and landscapes. Geographic modeling systems (GMS) allow us to formally define how we believe the watershed works. GIS is commonly accepted and often required by watershed managers. Acceptance and use of GMS technologies is growing among management groups to test the consequences of alter- ative land management scenarios.

Approaches of GIS application in watershed management

The integrated approach of GIS and Remote Sensing is being recognized universally as the unique highly effective and extremely versatile technology for evaluation, management and monitoring of natural resources and environment. With the concept of multidisciplinary integrated approach got an impetus in monitoring and management of resources and environment.

Groundwater modeling in watershed

GIS applications are beneficial in terms of watershed management issues, such as locating possible sites suitable for groundwater recharge, because:

A. A large amount of the information required (soils, land-use, and slope maps) to evaluate potential recharge sites currently exists in digital format.
B. GIS allows a great number of factors to be viewed on uniform media.
C. GIS has the ability to update information on features and corresponding data. This is essential for water resource management projects
D. A GIS database provides decision-makers with a comprehensive visual and tabular means for analyses on which to construct and support decisions.
E. Utility of this type of database would be for regional and city planners as well as for water supply and water quality monitoring.

Groundwater modeling is an attempt to replicate the behaviors of natural groundwater or hydrologic system by defining the essential features of the system in some controlled phys- ical or mathematical manner. Modeling plays an extremely important role in the management of hydrologic and groundwater system.

Remote sensing

Remote sensing is the science and art of obtaining information about a phenomenoa without being in contact with it. Remote sensing deals with the detection and measurement of phenomena with devices sensitive to elecromag- netic energy such as:

- Light (cameras and scanners)
- Heat (thermal scanners)
- Radio Waves (radar)
- Global positioning systems (GPS)

The NAVSTAR GPS (NAVigation Satellite Timing and Ranging) Global Positioning System (GPS) is a space-based radio-navigation and time transfer system. It is an all-weather system operated by the Department of Defense and is available world-wide 24 hours a day.

Top ten watershed lessons learned

- The Best Plans Have Clear Visions, Goals, and Action Items
- Good Leaders are Committed and Empower Others
- Having a Coordinator at the Watershed Level is Desirable
- Environmental, Economic, and Social Values are Compatible
- Plans Only Succeed if Implemented
- Partnerships Equal Power
- Good Tools Are Available
- Measure, Communicate, and Account for Progress
- Education and Involvement Drive Action
- Build on Small Successes

The Future of GIS Development

Many disciplines can benefit from GIS techniques. An active GIS market has resulted in lower costs and continual improvements in the hardware and software components of GIS. These developments will, in turn, result in a much wider application of the technology throughout government, business, and industry.

Global change and climate history program

Maps have traditionally been used to explore the Earth and to exploit its resources. GIS technology, as an expansion of cartographic science, has enhanced the efficiency and analytic power of traditional mapping. Now, as the scientific community recognizes the environm- ental consequences of human activity, GIS technology is becoming an essential tool in the effort to understand the process of global change. Various map and satellite information sources can be combined in modes that simulate the interactions of complex natural systems. Through a function known as visualization, a GIS can be used to produce images - not just maps, but drawings, animations, and other cart- ographic products.

These images allow resear- chers to view their subjects in ways that literally never have been seen before. The images often are equally helpful in conveying the technical concepts of GIS study subjects to non-scientists.

Adding the element of time

The condition of the Earth's surface, atmosphere, and subsurface can be examined by feeding satellite data into a GIS. GIS technology gives researchers the ability to examine the variations in Earth processes over days, months, and years. As an example, the changes in vegetation vigor through a growing season can be animated to determine when drought was most extensive in a particular region. The resulting graphic, known as a normalized veget-ation index, represents a rough measure of plant health. Working with two variables over time will allow researchers to detect regional differences in the lag between a decline in rainfall and its effect on vegetation. These analyses are made possible both by GIS technology and by the availability of digital data on regional and global scales. The satellite sensor output used to generate the vegetation graphic is produced by the Advanced Very High Resolution Radiometer or AVHRR. This sensor system detects the amounts of energy reflected from the Earth's surface across various bands of the spectrum for surface areas of about 1 square kilometer. The satellite sensor produces images of a particular location on the Earth twice a day. AVHRR is only one of many sensor systems used for Earth surface analysis. More sensors will follow, generating ever-greater amounts of data. GIS and related technology will help greatly in the management and analysis of these large volumes of data, allowing for better understanding of terrestrial processes and better management of human activities to maintain world economic vitality and environmental quality. GIS could shape the future of the field of watershed management in that it allows the managers to provide communities with the tools to be informed of their watershed situation, and to realize the impacts of various actions. Citizens will be able to make decisions and take actions toward maintaining and monitoring a productive watershed system.

MR. PAWAR RAJENDRA ANNA MR. SONAWANE AKASH SANKAR MS.
TRIBHUVAN LEENA KERU

Integrated watershed development plans

HISTORY AND EVOLUTION OFWATERSHED MANAGEMENT

Since the advent of civilization, water has always been the most important natural resource. Due to limited availability of fresh water, its proper management has always been of considerable importance. It has now assumed considerable significance due to phenomenal rise in its demand due to ever growing population. Earliest water related activities mainly aimed at controlling torrents in steep unstable mountainous areas with particular emphasis to minimize losses due to floods. The damage and destruction due to uncontrolled water flows were considered more important than the water shortages. In order to control water flow, water storage structures were evolved leading to the development of irrigation systems. The water storage structures faced siltation problems thereby seriously reducing their capacity. In order to overcome this problem, the soil conservation measures were employed to control soil erosion in the watershed. Full exploitation of the potential of watershed technology began in the beginning of modem era. Since Second World War, watershed management has become a subject of great international interest. Initially, the watershed management concept was introduced in a top-down approach with major emphasis to implement the soil and water conservation measures. In the absence of direct and immediate benefits of soil and water conservation measures, the participation of the watershed community could not be ensured which is so essential for the success of watershed projects. This led to a paradigm shift to the concept of watershed management. The top-down approach of implementing soil and water conservation measures was replaced by bottom-up approach to ensure creation of a self-supporting system essential for sustainability of the watershed. While carrying out watershed development activities, it has to be ensured that natural resources of watershed particularly soil and water are not adversely affected and ecological balance is not disturbed. A number of national and international organizations are engaged in activities related to watershed management such as Food and Agriculture Organization(FAO), International Association of Scientific Hydrology, International Union for Conservation of Nature and Natural Resources, International Union of Forest Research 'Organization, World Meteorological Organization, etc.

Watershed Development in India

Watershed activities with respect to hydrological monitoring were initiated in 42 small watersheds located in 8 Centres of Central Soil and Water ConservationResearch and Training Institute (CSWCRTI) in 1956. Subsequently watershed based Operational Research Projects (ORPs) were taken up in different parts of the country in 1974, in order to reduce soil loss, increase water availability so as to enhance cropping intensity, agricultural productivity and generate employment.The central and state governments have undertaken various developmentprogrammes based on watershed approach as outline below. The Ministry of Rural Development, Government of India is a front runner in these efforts and has implemented special area development programmes for water harvesting.

Soil Conservation in Catchment of River Valley Project

The programme was initiated during the Third Five Year Plan to treat catchment area for reducing silt production rate and subsequent siltation of reservoirs, checking soil erosion and consequently improving agricultural productivity. The programme is being implemented in 27 watersheds covering 17 states including Damodar Valley Corporation area. Soil and water conservation measures are also being adopted in critically degraded watersheds ranging between 2,000 and 4,000 ha area.

Integrated Agricultural Development in Drought Prone Areas

Rain fed farming is totally dependent on unreliable and widely variable rainfall resulting in very low agricultural productivity. Monsoon failure further complicates the situation causing unbearable misery and suffering to the people. The Drought Prone Area Programme (DPAP) of Government of India aimed at promoting integrated agricultural development in dry farming regions based on ecologically balanced approach instead of providing temporary relief. The programme also envisaged setting up of productive infrastructure for providing immediate employment in emergencies to the weaker sections. In this programme, a planned methodology in terms of detailed soil survey, hydrological survey and topographic survey was proposed for preparation of the master plan. Based on this, activities such as land use capability classification, installation of wells depending up on existing conditions of the area; water harvesting programmes (construction of tanks or check dams in the catchment areas etc.) were intended.

Desert Development Programme

(DDP) The programme was initiated in 1977-78 to control desertification of the desert area by integrating and linking other related state/central programmes and conserve and harness land, water and other natural resources including rainfall for restoration of long term ecological balance. The programme aims at achieving afforestation with special emphasis on sand dune stabilization and shelter belt plantation and grassland development, soil and moisture conservation and. water resources development. This programme fully financed by the central government covered about 36.2 m ha of 131 blocks of 21 districts in five states namely Rajasthan, Haryana, Gujarat (hot arid region), Jammu and Kashmir and Himachal Pradesh (cold arid region).

Himalayan Watershed Management

Project in Uttar Pradesh Himalayan watershed management project funded by the World Bank was taken up in 1983 in two watersheds namely Nayar in Garhwal and Panarin Kumaon regions in Uttarakhand's covering an area of 2.47 lakh ha. It aimed at minimizing further deterioration of the Himalayan eco-system caused by depletion of forest cover, over grazing, awful land use and careless road construction.

Operational Research Projects on Integrated Watershed Management

These projects were taken up in 47 watersheds spread over 16 states (Andhra Pradesh, Bihar, Gujarat, Haryana, Madhya Pradesh, Maharashtra, Orissa, Punjab, Himachal Pradesh), Jammu and Kashmir, Karnataka, Kerala, Rajasthan, Tamil Nadu, Uttar Pradesh and West Bengal) in 1983 covering an area of 35739 ha with the financial assistance of Ministry of Agriculture and Rural Development, Government of India and under the technical guidance of Indian Council of Agricultural Research (ICAR). The projects aimed at developing a programme with people' participation for arresting the deterioration of environment and building up permanent assets in the form of water, sustainable vegetation and improved productivity of cropped land.

National Watershed Development Programme of Rain fed Agriculture(NWDPRA)

The programme initiated in 1986-87 in the unirrigated arable lands in 25 states mostly had rainfall ranging between 500 and 1125 mm and more. The districts with over 30 % area under irrigation were usually excluded. The programme was restructured in the Eight Five Year Plan in order to achieve sustainable production of bio-mass as well as restoration of ecological balance in the vast rain fed areas of the country. It mainly focused on conservation and utilization of land, water, plant, animal and human resources in a harmonious and integrated manner with low-cost, simple, effective and replicable technology, generation of massive employment and reduction of inequalities between irrigated and rain fed areas.

The main activities of the project included:

- Land and moisture management including optimal cropping system, dry land horticulture, fodder production and farm forestry;
- Contingency seed and planting material stocking;
- Training, seminars, study tours for staff and farmers within the state/regional! National level;
- Adoptive research trials on different crops in small and marginal farmers land;

- Procurement, fabrication-and supply of survey equipment and prototype implements; and
- Preparation of field manuals and publicity materials.

The programme has been able to achieve the following:

- unified command approach of multi-disciplinary team for effective Organizational set-up for effective implementation of watershed development programmes;
- Increased productivity of different crops in both black and red soil regions' by contour farming;
- Significant in situ moisture conservation, cropping intensity and productivity in different farming systems based on contour vegetative barriers.

Integrated Wasteland Development Programme (IWDP)

The programme initiated in 1989 aimed at developing wastelands on a watershed basis and mainly focused on silvi-pasture and soil moisture conservation on wastelands.

Integrated Watershed Management in the Catchments of Flood Prone

Rivers

The programme was undertaken during Fourth Five Year Plan in eight flood prone rivers of Gangetic basin namely, Ajoy, Gomti, Punpun, RoopNaraian, Sahibi, Sone, Upper Ganga and Upper Yamuna covering watershed area of 16.7 million ha spread over the states of Bihar, Haryana, Himachal Pradesh, Madhya Pradesh, Rajasthan, Uttar Pradesh, West Bengal and Union Territory of Delhi. The programme aimed at enhancing ability of the watershed by absorbing large amount of rainwater, reducing erosion and consequent silt load in rivers and thus mitigating the effect of floods in productive plains.

Integrated Watershed Development Project for Hills and Plains

The World Bank projects in Himachal Pradesh, Jammu and Kashmir, Punjab and Haryana covering an area of 1.24 lakh ha aimed at slowing and reversing degradation of the natural environment through the use of appropriate soil and water conservation practices.

Integrated Watershed Development Project (Plains)

The World Bank project covering an area of 4.331akh ha in Gujarat, Orissa and Rajasthan aimed at slowing down and reversing ecological degradation in a variety of agro-ecological zones by promoting sustainable and replicable production system.

Other Watershed Management Projects

Internationally funded watershed management projects are also being implemented in the country.

GUIDELINES FOR WATERSHED PROGRAMMES

In 1994-95, Ministry of Rural Areas and Employment, Government of India came up with strict guidelines for watershed programmes to achieve optimum utilization of the watershed's natural resources, employment generation and over all socioeconomic development. Subsequently, Ministry of Rural Development revised the guidelines in 2001 to make them more focused, transparent and easy to follow. The guidelines for watershed development provided a detailed institutional framework at all levels of implementation, particularly people organizations called the Watershed Association, the Watershed Committee, the Self Help Groups, the User Groups at the village level. The guidelines were further refined with the launch of new initiative "Hariyali" in 2003. Hariyali sought to empower Panchayat Raj Institutions (PRIs) both administratively and financially in the implementation of the watershed development programmes. The guidelines for Hariyali wereapplicable to IWDP, DPAP, DDP and any other programme notified by the GOl. Common Guidelines for Watershed Development Projects were issued by the Department of Land Resources, Ministry of Rural Development in 2008 and are based on the following features:

Equity and Gender Sensitivity:

Watershed Development Projects should be considered as levers of inclusiveness. Project hnplementing Agencies must facilitate the equity processes such as (a) enhanced livelihood opportunities for the poor through investment in their assets and improvements in productivity and income, (b) improving access of the poor, especially women to the benefits, (c) enhancing role of women in decision-making processes and their representation in the institutional arrangements and (d) ensuring access to usufruct (legal) rights from the common property resources for the resource poor.

Decentralization:

Project management would improve with decentralization, delegation and professionalism. Establishing suitable institutional arrangements within the overall framework of the Panchayati Raj Institutions and the operational flexibility in norms to suit varying local conditions will enhance decentralization. Empowered committees with delegation to rationalize the policies, continuity in administrative support and timely release of funds are the other instruments for effective decentralization.

Facilitating Agencies:

Social mobilization, community organization, capacities building of communities in planning and implementation, ensuring equity arrangements etc. need intensive facilitation. Competent organizations including voluntary organizations with professional teams having necessary skills and expertise would be selected through a rigorous process and may be provided financial support to perform the above specific. Functions.

Centrality of Community Participation:

Involvement of primary stakeholders is at the centre of planning, budgeting, implementation and management of watershed projects. Community organizations may be closely associated with and accountable to Gram Sabhas in project activities.

Capacity Building and Technology Inputs:

Considerable stress would be given on capacity building as a crucial component for achieving the desired results. This would be a continuous process enabling functionaries to enhance their knowledge and skills and develop the correct orientation and perspectives thereby becoming more effective in performing their roles and responsibilities. With current trends and advances in information technology and remote sensing, it is possible to acquire detailed information about the various field level characteristics of any area or region. Thus, the endeavor would be to build in strong technology inputs into the new vision of watershed programmes.

Monitoring, Evaluation and Learning:

A participatory, outcome and impact oriented and user-focused monitoring, evaluation and learning system would be put in place to obtain feedback and undertake improvements in planning, project design and implementation.

Organizational Restructuring:

Establishing appropriate technical and professional support structures at national, state, district and project levels and developing effective functional partnerships among project authorities, implementing agencies and support organizations would play a vital role.

WATERSHED MANAGEMENT ACTION PLAN

Watershed management action plan needs to be prepared for all the arable and non-arable lands including degraded forestlands, government and community lands and private lands. The following activities may have to be incorporated in the action plan depending up on agro-climatic conditions of the region as well as socio-economic condition of people:

- Development of small water harvesting structures such as low-cost farm ponds, nalla bunds, check-dams, percolation tanks and other groundwater recharge measures;
- Renovation and augmentation of water sources, desiltation of village tanks for drinking water/ irrigation! Fisheries development;

- Fisheries development in village ponds/tanks, farm ponds etc;
- Afforestation including, block plantations, agro- forestry and horticultural development, shelterbelt plantations, sand dune stabilization etc;
- Pasture development either by itself or in conjunction with plantations;
- Land Development including in situ soil and moisture conservation measures like contour and graded bunds equipped with plantation, bench terracing hilly terrain, nursery raising for fodder, timber, fuel wood, horticulture and non-timber forest product species;
- Drainage line treatment with a combination of vegetative and engineering structures;
- Repair, restoration and up-gradation of existing common property assets and structures in the watershed to obtain optimum and sustained benefits from previous public investments;
- Crop demonstrations for popularizing new crops/varieties or innovative management practices; and
- Promotion and propagation of non-conventional energy saving devices, energy conservation measures, bio-fuel plantations etc.

Design of Tanks and Ponds for Water Harvesting
Percolation Tank

A percolation tank is generally constructed in low level wasteland or a small drain. It has well defined catchment and the water spilling over is diverted to a nearby natural drain. It consists of earthen embankment and an overflow type masonry waste weir. Permeable formation in the reservoir bed is an essential requirement of percolation tank. The tank acts as storage of intercepted runoff, which percolates down to phreatic aquifer creating a recharge mound. The percolation time depends upon the permeability of bed formation. Normally it is expected that between two consecutive rains spells, most of the storage percolates down. Thus, during 2 to 3 rainfall cycles, the actual recharge gain is two to three times the storage capacity of the tank. The shape and size of the recharge mound depends on the nature of phreatic aquifer underlying the surface. This type of recharge structure is useful in area having sandstone and limestone formation underlying.

Tank is a general term used for surface water storage of moderate size. The storage may have come into being due to interception of rainwater in a natural depression or a manmade excavation. Such water bodies are popularly called ponds. Alternatively water storage may be done by closing the openings of a natural saucer shaped landform by constructing bund sized embankments. The storage so created is called a tank. The tank bunds are mostly constructed with earth to keep cost of construction low and are commensurate with the benefits envisaged.

Water storages of large size are not called tanks, but they are referred to as reservoirs. Such reservoirs are formed in the river valleys by constructing a barrier or a dam using masonry, concrete or earth depending upon site conditions. Technically, bund is a miniature form of a dam.

Due to simplicity in construction it was a very popular mode of conserving rainwater. In South India where rivers are monsoon fed, tanks assume special importance. In the plains of Uttar Pradesh, West Bengal and Orissa as also in the plateaus of Madhya Pradesh, Chhattisgarh tanks have been extensively practiced.

Classification of Tanks

Bunds which are generally less than 12 m high, results in tanks. From the consideration of height of bunds, up to 4.5 m high bunds generate a small tank. Medium sized tanks are formed by bunds up to 9 m height. It may however be noted that, this classification is very approximate because the shape and size of the tank is not dependent on the height of the bund alone. It is equally influenced by the topographical features of the region.

Network of Tanks

The tank system may exist with each tank as a separate entity or in the form of a group of tanks in a series or tanks with inter-connection. In a tank system, following types of network exist:

(i) Isolated tanks;

(ii) Tanks with inter-connections; and

(iii) Tanks in series.

Isolated Tanks: When a tank is fed by an independent free draining catchment and also when the surplus flows do not form network inflow into another tank, the tank system is called an isolated tank system. Mostly large and medium sized tanks are constructed as isolated tanks with independent catchment area. Also in the plains and on plateau lands, tanks exist in isolation.

Tanks with Inter-Connections: Sometimes a group of tanks may be so situated that they could be inter-connected to receive flows through, as well as deliver flows to other tanks in the group severally. It thereby implies that the tanks have a combined catchment. Any surplus water received by a tank from the catchment lying above it is transferred to other tanks. Depending upon the prevailing hydro-meteorological conditions, the tanks are capable of feeding either each other or one another. Thus, optimum water utilization and storage is achieved.

Tank in Series: Such tanks are located alongside the river drainage channels. They are fed by inflow drains and serviced by escape or outflow drains. The tanks in upper reaches get their supplies from the catchment through inflowing drains. It then lets its surplus flow down through an escape or outflow drain, which contributes to the inflow of the tank lower down in the series. Thus while the uppermost tanks have substantially free catchment, the tanks lower down have limited free catchment falling between two tanks. The tanks lower down in the series get inflows immediately after rainfall from their free draining catchments. But supplies from already intercepted catchments are received only after the upper tanks get filled. The advantage of this system is that, surplus water from the upper tank is picked up by the lower tanks rather than allowing any wastage.

However, there is a safety related disadvantage. In case of breach in the upper tank, lower tanks also become prone to severe flooding endangering the safety of the tank bunds. To avoid this, breaching sections are provided at appropriate locations in each tank.

Water Harvesting by Ponds

The traditional practice of collection rainwater in village ponds suffers from following limitations:

- Large open surface is subjected to high evaporation losses.
- Large bed area is subjected to high seepage losses.

In Spite of these limitations in the village ponds, the bulk water requirement for about half the year is met from them. Small groundwater recharge mound formed under the pond bed used to partially supply through wells dug in the pond bed. This traditionally practiced rainwater harvesting structures have served water supply requirements since ages. During the scarcity years, some deepening of ponds is made through de-silting. But if it is done in a haphazard manner, it does not help much and rather it may lead to other problems like water logging, mosquito breeding, etc.

Pond Lining

The limitations of traditional ponds, especially the quality deterioration and seepage losses could be completely stopped by using plastic lining. This simple technique has proved to be effective. The evaporation loss could be checked by use of chemical retardants and adopting system of multiple ponds system (i.e., compartments). Limitation of the depth factor has to be accepted and required storage could be built by increasing the length and breadth of the pond. Of course, in places where salty water is available is at greater depths, the pond storage can be increased even with less open surface and thereby reducing the evaporation losses. Such favorable locations may not be provided with plastic lining, provided the rate of salt contamination from the sediments is within the limits. Plastic lining is a rather costly proposition, however, it envisages better use of local water resources and regular maintenance is almost negligible.

This technology involves lining of the walls and floor of the pond, tank reservoir with tough, wide-width low-density polyethylene (LDPE) film. These LDPE films are available in widths of 4 to 12 m and thickness of 100 to 250 microns. These films meet specifications as per the Bureau of Indian Standards Code IS: 2508 - 1984. This film has excellent water barrier properties, very good blend of physical properties such as tensile impact strength coupled with good weathering capability and chemical resistance properties. These films also prevent the inherent salinity of the soils and saline groundwater from seeping into the pond or tank and start contamination.

The construction of plastic lined pond includes excavation work, screening work for removing big boulders and sharp edged gravels which could damage the plastic film, dressing of sides and beds so that lining is not punctured, laying plastic film on beds and sides, brick lining on the sidewalls, soil filling on the floor, inlet system and distribution system. By 2008, 19 villages of Bhal area of Gujarat, India had 20 such plastic lined ponds

Definition of Land Capability

Land capability may be defined as the ability of the land surface to support natural plant growth/ wildlife habitat or artificial crop growth/ human habitat. Thus, it indicates the type of land use [viz., human habitation, agriculture, pastures, forests, wildlife habitat, etc.] that is suitable over a particular type of land. Different lands have different capabilities depending on the land characteristics like slope, soil type, soil depth and erosion conditions. If certain land characteristics are not conducive for agriculture, it is desirable to utilize or ensure the continuity of that land area for other land uses as mentioned earlier.

The ultimate goal of allocation of various land capabilities over a vast land area with varied characteristics is to achieve complete soil conservation. Complete soil conservation implies perfect soil health and zero soil erosion on a sustained basis. It also facilitates total water conservation and total vegetation conservation. Thereby it results in integrated watershed management on a long term basis.

In the next section, we shall discuss the classification of land capability based on the land characteristics. This land capability classification should ensure appropriate land use for every land area for peaceful coexistence of different flora and fauna including human habitation and also a sustained productivity through human activities.

Classification of Land Capability

The Soil Conservation Service (SCS) of the United States Department of Agriculture (USDA) has done a pioneering work on land capability classification [Klingbiel and Montgomery, 1961]. According to that, the land capability is classified broadly into two groups based on the cultivability of the land. The first group consisting of all the lands which are suitable for cultivation is referred to as 'Group 1 Lands'. The remaining group consisting of all the lands which are unsuitable for cultivation is referred to as 'Group 2 Lands'. Each of these two groups are further classified into four classes. Thus 'Group 1 Lands' comprise 'Land Classes I to IV' which are cultivable and 'Group 2 Lands' comprise 'Land Classes V to VIII' which are non-cultivable.

The following paragraphs describe each of the two groups and eight land classes in terms of their land characteristics and land use:

Group 1 Lands: Generally Suitable for Cultivation

Class I Lands: These lands are nearly level with slopes generally within 1%. The soils are deep, fertile, easily workable and are not subjected to damaging overflows. There are hardly any restrictions or limitations for their use. These lands are very good lands which can be safely cultivated by using any farming method to grow any crop, even intensively also. However, proper crop rotation and green manure use should be followed to maintain soil fertility [Mal, 1994].

Class II Lands: These lands generally have gentle slope in the range of 1 to 3%. They can be easily cultivated with some conservation practices like contour farming, strip cropping, bund construction or terracing. Therefore one or more of the following limitations exist which slightly reduce the crop choice:

- Moderate susceptibility to erosion by wind or water;
- Less than ideal soil depth;
- Somewhat unfavorable soil structure and workability;
- Slight to moderate salinity;
- Occasionally damaging overflows;
- Wetness existing permanently which can be corrected by drainage; and
- Slight climatic limitations on land use and management.

Class III Lands: These lands generally have slopes in the range of 3 to 5% and therefore have severe limitations which further reduce the crop choice or require special conservation practices [like contour farming, strip cropping, cover cropping, bund construction or terracing] or both. Lands in this class have more restrictions than those in Class II Lands due to land characteristics. All the limitations of Class II Lands are applicable here also, but to a greater extent. Hay or pasture crops that completely cover the soil should be preferred. On wet lands of this Class -which usually have heavy and slowly permeable soils, a drainage system along with a suitable cropping plan to improve the soil structure is required.

Class IV Lands: These lands have fairly good soils [i. e., having shallow soil depth and low fertility] and generally have somewhat steep slopes in the range of 5 to 8%. Therefore they have either very severe limitations that largely restrict the crop choice or require very careful management or both. Lands may be suitable only for two to three common crops which build and maintain soil -like the fully covering pastures, with occasional grain crops which can be grown usually once in five years. These lands may have one or more of the following permanent features:

- Heavy susceptibility for erosion due to wind, water with severe effects of past erosion;2. Low moisture holding capacity;

- Frequent overflows accompanied by severe crop damage;
- Water logging, excessive wetness and severe salinity; and
- Moderately adverse climate.

Land Capability Sub-Classes: Lands in Classes II, III and IV are further categorised into sub-classes based on the following limitations:

- Risk of erosion or past erosion damage is designated by the symbol 'e';
- Wetness damage or overflow is designated by the symbol 'w';
- Soil root zone limitations are denoted by 's'; and
- Climatic limitations are designated by 'c'.

Group 2 Lands: Generally Not Suitable for Cultivation

Class V Lands: These lands generally have slopes in the range of 8 to 12%. They usually have no to little erosion hazard but have other limitations which restrict their use mainly to pastures, forests, wildlife food and cover. Controlled grazing may be permitted. Some of the examples of Class V Lands are:

- Bottom lands subject to frequent overflows that prevent the normal production of cultivated crops;
- Stony or rocky lands;
- Few ponded areas where soils are suitable for grasses or trees.

Class VI Lands: The lands in this Class have shallow soils and generally have quite steep slopes ranging to 18%. They have severe limitations which restrict their use to pastures with very limited grazing, woodlands, wildlife food and cover. Some of the limitations of these lands which can't be corrected are:

- Severe erosion;
- Stony texture with shallow rocks
- Excessive wetness or overflow

- Low moisture capacity
- Severe climate.

Class VII Lands: The lands in this Class are generally eroded, rough, having shallow soil depth and steeper slopes ranging to 25%. The soils may be swampy or drought prone, with all the limitations of Class VI Lands even to a higher degree. If there is good rainfall, they may be used for forestry with fully green cover, gully control structures and severely restricted grazing.

Class VIII Lands: These lands are rough with probably the worst soil types and possibly the steepest slopes in excess of 25%. They can only be used with very sound gully control measures for forests –if conducive for tree growth, and also for wildlife habitat. However, tree felling and grazing should be strictly avoided.

Importance of watershed management in national development

- National Level
- State Level
- District Level
- Panchayati Raj Institutions (PRIs)

National Level

The National Rainfed Area Authority (NRAA), a nodal agency at the central level facilitates budgetary allocation and smooth flow of funds from different projects of Government of India to the District Watershed Development Units (DWDU) for speedy and successful implementation of these watershed development projects. It acts as an effective coordinating mechanism between different ministries, Organizations and departments responsible for undertaking watershed development programmes. It is also responsible for supporting the process of preparing strategic plans for watershed development projects at the state and district levels keeping in view the specific agro-climatic and socio-economic conditions. It also supports state level nodal agencies in identifying resource organizations and establishing capacity building arrangements. The professional multi-disciplinary experts in the field of agriculture, water management, institutionand capacity building etc. Constitute the nodal agency.

State Level

A State Level Nodal Agency (SLNA) is empowered to oversee all watershed projects in the state based on the approved perspective and strategic plan. The SLNA is headed by the Development Commissioner/Additional Chief Secretary/agricultural Production Commissioner/Principal secretary and comprises of onerepresentative from National Bank for Agriculture and Rural Development(NABARD), one representative each from the state department of rural development, agriculture, animal husbandry and allied sectors, one representative from groundwater board, one representative from voluntary organization and two experts from research institutes / state universities, National Rural Employment Guarantee Schemes (NREGS), Backward Regions Grand Fund (BRGF) and other related implementing agencies are also represented. A team of four to seven professional expertsin the field of agriculture, water management, capacity building,social science, information technology, administration, accounts etc. assist the SLNA which provides technical supports to District Watershed Development Unit (DWDU). It also prepares perspective and strategic plans of watershed for the state on the basis of plans prepared at the block and the district levels. It also sets the expected outputs and financial outlays based on which approval of central nodal agencies is sought. It also establishes monitoring and evaluation of the watershed projects.

District Level

District Watershed Development Unit (DWDU) is established to oversee the implementation of watershed projects in each district with separate accounts. It functions in close coordination with District Planning Committee (DPC) with a representative each of NRGA and BRGF at the district level. The DWDU comprising of a full time project manager and three to four experts on agriculture, water management, social science, management and accounts and is responsible for identifying potential Project Implementing Agencies (PIAs). It also facilitates preparation of district strategic and action plans including capacity building and ensures smooth flow of funds to the projects and timely submission of required documents to SLNA. It also facilitates coordination with relevant programmers of agriculture, horticulture, rural development, animal husbandry, etc. with the watershed projects for enhancing productivity and livelihood opportunities.

Panchayati Raj Institutions (PRIs)

Panchayati Raj Institutions (PRIs) are actively involved in the watershed programmes. The District Panchayat-Zila Parishad are entrusted with the responsibility of coordinating various sectoralschemes with watershed development projects, review of progress, settling disputes etc. Intermediate Panchayats have an important role in planning the watershed development projects at the intermediate level and provide support to PIAs and Gram Panchayats Watershed Committees in technical guidance with the help of their subject matter specialists.

Project Implementation Agency (PIA)

The PIAs include relevant line departments, autonomous organizations under state/ central governments, government institutes/research bodies, intermediate panchayats and voluntary organizations (VOs). VOs have an important role in creating awareness, capacity building, information, education and communication and social audit. Each PIA is supported by a dedicated watershed development team (WDT) with the approval of DWDU. The Project Implementing Agency (PIA) provides necessary technical guidance to the Gram Panchayat for preparation of development plans for the watershed through Participatory Rural Appraisal (PRA) exercise, undertake community organization andtraining for the village communities, supervise watershed development activities, inspect and authenticate project accounts, encourage adoption of low cost technologies and build upon indigenous technical knowledge, monitor and review the overall project implementation and set up institutional arrangements for post-project operation and maintenance and further development of the assets created during the project period. It also facilitates the mobilization of additional financial resources from other government programmes, such as NREGA, BRGF, SGRY, National Horticulture Mission, Tribal Welfare Schemes, Artificial Groundwater Recharging, Greening India, etc.

Watershed Development Team

WDT comprises of at-least four experts preferably with professional degree in the disciplines of agriculture, soil science, water management, social mobilization and institutional building. At least one of the WDT members should be a woman. The WDT should be located as close as possible to the watershed project and its close collaboration with the team of experts at the district and state level must be ensured. It guides WC in the formulation of the watershed action plan. It assists Gram Panchayat Gram Sabha in constitution of the WC, User Groups (UGs) and Self-Help Groups (SHGs). The User Groups deal with homogeneous group ofpersons having land within the watershed areas while SHGs include small and marginal farmers households, landless, labours, women and SC/ST persons. It also ensures active participation of women, conducts participatory base-line surveys, training and capacity building, prepare resource development plans. It prepares Detailed Project Report (DPR) for the consideration of Gram Sabha and facilitates the development of livelihood opportunities for the landless and maintaining project accounts.

Panchayati Raj Institutions (PRIs)

Panchayati Raj Institutions (PRIs) are actively involved in the watershed programmes. The District PanchayatJZila Parishad are entrusted with the responsibility of coordinating various sectoralschemes with watershed development projects, review of progress, settling disputes etc. Intermediate Panchayats have an important role in planning the watershed development projects at the intermediate level and provide support to PIAs and Gram PanchayatsIWatershed Committees in technical guidance with the help of the subject matter specialists.The Zila Parish ads and other Panchayati Raj Institutions (PRIs) shall have very important role to play in watershed development programmes. Wherever the DRDA has been made responsible for implementation of the watershed programmes, the Chief Executive Officer of the Zila Parishad shall be a member of the DWDC. The PRIs shall have the right to monitor and review the implementation of the programme and provide guidance for improvements in the administrative arrangements and procedures with a view to ensure convergence of other programmes of Ministry of Rural Development such as JGSY, SGSY, lAY, CRSP, Rural Drinking Water Supply etc.

References

- Water and soil management for water conservation in watershed - S. O. Hur*, K. H. Jung, Y. K. Sonn, S. Y. Hong, and S. K. Ha (Soil Management Division, National Institute of Agricultural Science & Technology Rural Development Administration, Suwon, Korea)
- Water and Soil Conservation Chairperson - Father Hermann Bacher, Chairman - WOTR, Ahmednagar Co-ordinator – (Dr.Prashant Nichal, Director Soil Conservation & Watershed Management)
- Soil and Water Conservation of Manimuktha Watershed – A Case Study Dr. N. Nagarajan , Dr. S. Poongothai, Dr. S. Ramesh, Mr. Santhakumar Swamidurai
- Soil Conservation and Watershed Management Programs/ Activities Ministry of Forests and Soil Conservation Department of Soil Conservation and Watershed Management
- Soil and Water Conservation Directorate of Forests Government of West Bengal
- Water Harvesting and Soil Conservation in High Rainfall Areas (North Bengal Terai Development Project Government of West Bengal)
- Study on Impact Assessment of Soil and Water Conservation Measures Implemented in Swan Catchment (Swan River Integrated Watershed Management Project (SRIWMP), Una, Himachal Pradesh)
- **Concept of Watershed Management and its Components** G.N. Gurjar, N. K. Meena1, Sanjay Swami2, S. G. Telkar3, E. A. S. Lyngdoh Ph.D. Scholar at CPGS, Umiam, Meghalaya-793103 Associate Professor, SNRM, CPGS, Umiam, Meghalaya Assistant Professor, Dept. of Agriculture, Jagannath University, Chaksu, Jaipur-303 90

MuffakhamJah College of Engineering and Technology

- Hydrologic Processes and Watershed Respons (Rita D. Winkler, R.D. (Dan) Moore, Todd E. Redding, David L. Spittlehouse, Darryl E. Carlyle-Moses, and Brian D. Smerdon).
- Watershed Hydrology: Scientific Advances and Environmental Assessments
- Watershed hydrological modelling in data scarce regions; integratingecohydrology and regionalization for the southern Caspian Sea basin, Iran
- RAINFALL-RUNOFF PROCESSES David G. Tarboton A workbook to accompany the Rainfall-Runoff Processes Web module.
- Water relations and hydrologic cycles R. H. WARING, JAMES J. ROGERS, & W. T. SWANK
- A taxonomy of hydrological processes and watershed function Hilary (McMillan1 ,1San Diego State University)
- Hydrological Modeling As A Tool For Sustainable Water Resources Management: A Case Study Of The Awash River Basin (Selome M. Tessema)
- Soil and Water Conservation of Manimuktha Watershed – A Case Study (Dr. N. Nagarajan *, Dr. S. Poongothai, Dr. S. Ramesh, Mr. Santhakumar Swamidurai)
- Soil and Water Conservation Engineering Measures for Treatment of Arable Land in Watershed (Dr. Bhupendra Singh Naik).
- Application of Remote Sensing & GIS In Watershed Prioritization, Development Planning & Monitoring K.Ganesha Raj & V S HegdeNNRMS/EOS, ISRO HQ,AntarikshBhavan, New BEL Road,Bangalore-560 094.
- GIS and Remote Sensing Applications for Watershed Planning in the Maumee River Basin, Ohio Kevin Czajkowski and Patrick L. Lawrence.

- Automatic Watershed Delineation using Remote Sensingand Geographic Information System D.K.Tripathi Department of Geography, Kamla Nehru Institute of Physical & Social Sciences Sultanpur, UP,India.
- Overview of Remote Sensing and GIS Uses in Watershed and TMDL Analyses Nigel W. T. Quinn, Ph.D., P.E., D.WRE, F.ASCE (Research Group Leader, Hydro-Ecological Engineering Advanced DecisionSupport, Berkeley National Laboratory)
- Watershed management in Afghanistan: Lessons from South AsiaAuthor links open overlay panel. RatnaReddy
  - Prioritization of Watershed Using Remote Sensing and Geographic Information System Devendra Kumar